ROUTLEDGE LIBRARY EDITIONS:
ARISTOTLE

Volume 7

THE STRUCTURE OF
ARISTOTELIAN LOGIC

THE STRUCTURE OF
ARISTOTELIAN LOGIC

JAMES WILKINSON MILLER

LONDON AND NEW YORK

First published in 1938

This edition first published in 2016
by Routledge
2 Park Square, Milton Park, Abingdon, Oxon OX14 4RN

and by Routledge
711 Third Avenue, New York, NY 10017

Routledge is an imprint of the Taylor & Francis Group, an informa business

© 1938 James Wilkinson Miller

All rights reserved. No part of this book may be reprinted or reproduced or utilised in any form or by any electronic, mechanical, or other means, now known or hereafter invented, including photocopying and recording, or in any information storage or retrieval system, without permission in writing from the publishers.

Trademark notice: Product or corporate names may be trademarks or registered trademarks, and are used only for identification and explanation without intent to infringe.

British Library Cataloguing in Publication Data
A catalogue record for this book is available from the British Library

ISBN: 978-1-138-92762-9 (Set)
ISBN: 978-1-315-67490-2 (Set) (ebk)
ISBN: 978-1-138-94232-5 (Volume 7) (hbk)
ISBN: 978-1-138-94242-4 (Volume 7) (pbk)
ISBN: 978-1-315-67319-6 (Volume 7) (ebk)

Publisher's Note
The publisher has gone to great lengths to ensure the quality of this reprint but points out that some imperfections in the original copies may be apparent.

Disclaimer
The publisher has made every effort to trace copyright holders and would welcome correspondence from those they have been unable to trace.

THE STRUCTURE OF ARISTOTELIAN LOGIC

BY

JAMES WILKINSON MILLER, Ph.D.

*Professor of Philosophy in the
College of William and Mary in Virginia*

PSYCHE MONOGRAPHS : No 11

KEGAN PAUL, TRENCH, TRUBNER & Co. Ltd.
Broadway House, Carter Lane, London, E.C.

1938

Printed in Great Britain by
R. I. SEVERS, CAMBRIDGE

CONTENTS

	PAGE
PREFACE	9
INTRODUCTION	11
1. Preliminary definition of Aristotelian logic	11
2. Exclusion of irrelevant material	12
3. The aim of this book	13
4. The problems of this book	13
5. The problem of systematization	13
6. The problem of the rules	14
7. The problem of interpretation	16
8. General conclusions	17
9. Appendix. Review of introductory Aristotelian logic	18
CHAPTER I. POSTULATES FOR ARISTOTELIAN LOGIC	25
10. Reduction as deduction	25
11. The general character of our systematization	28
12. Primitive ideas	30
13. Discussion of primitive ideas	30
14. Postulates of validity	30
15. Discussion of the postulates of validity	31
16. Postulate of invalidity	32
17. Discussion of the postulate of invalidity	32
18. Note on the postulates	32
19. Definitions	32
20. Discussion of definitions	32
21. Functions	32
CHAPTER II. IMMEDIATE INFERENCE	34
22. The manner of writing proofs	34
23. Substitution	34
24. The principles of eductive equivalence	35
25. The principles of double negation	36
26. The principles of contradiction	37
27. Table of propositional forms	37

28. Summary of the principles of equivalence . 37
29. Definition of eduction 39
30. The valid moods of eduction 39
31. The invalid moods of eduction. . . . 39
32. Summary of eduction 42
33. Alternative summary of eduction . . . 43
34. Definition of opposition 45
35. Theorems of opposition 45
36. Summary of opposition 45

CHAPTER III. MEDIATE INFERENCE 48
37. Definition of syllogism 48
38. The valid moods of the syllogism . . . 48
39. Consequences of postulate 1.5 48
40. Invalid moods of the syllogism . . . 49
41. Summary of the syllogism 52
42. Introduction to the sorites 52
43. Definition of the sorites 52
44. The sorites with three premises: valid moods . 53
45. The sorites with three premises: invalid moods 53
46. Introduction to the sorites with n premises . 55
47. Definitions 56
48. Summary of the valid kinds of sorites with n premises 57
49. Lemmas 59
50. Summary of the invalid kinds of sorites with n premises 60
51. The sorites: conclusion 62

CHAPTER IV. COMPLETION OF THE SYSTEM . . 63
52. Introduction 63
53. Normal *vs.* telescoped arguments . . . 63
54. The search for a new postulate . . . 65
55. Postulate set A 66
56. Postulate set B 67

CHAPTER V. DISTRIBUTION, QUALITY, AND QUANTITY . 68
57. Introduction 68
58. The doctrine of distribution 68

59. The contradiction	69
60. The source of the contradiction	70
61. Definition of distribution	70
62. The old table of distribution	71
63. The new table of distribution	72
64. Summary and transition	73
65. Strong versus weak distribution	73
66. Table of strong distribution	74
67. Table of weak distribution	74
68. Quality and quality-in-sense	74
69. Quantity	75

CHAPTER VI. THE RULES OF ARISTOTELIAN LOGIC . 76

70. Introduction to rules for eduction	76
71. Rules for eduction	77
72. Second set of rules for eduction	78
73. Third set of rules for eduction	78
74. Proof of the rules for eduction	79
75. Concerning rules for telescoped eduction	79
76. Introduction to rules for the syllogism	80
77. Rules for the syllogism	80
78. Second set of rules for the syllogism	81
79. Third set of rules for the syllogism	81
80. Proof of the rules for the syllogism	81
81. Introduction to rules for the sorites	81
82. Rules for the sorites	82
83. Second set of rules for the sorites	82
84. Third set of rules for the sorites	82
85. Proof of the rules for the sorites	82
86. General rules of inference	83
87. Telescoped syllogism and telescoped sorites	83

CHAPTER VII. INTERPRETATIONS OF ARISTOTELIAN LOGIC   84

88. Introduction	84
89. The search for an interpretation	85
90. Interpretation A	87
91. Interpretation B	89
92. Other proposed interpretations	90
93. Extension and intension	90

CONCLUSION 92
    94. Introduction 92
    95. Negative terms in Aristotelian logic . . . 92
    96. The correctness of Aristotelian logic . . 93
    97. Aristotelian versus modern logic . . . 93

INDEX 96

PREFACE

This book is a short treatise rather than a textbook and is addressed to advanced students of logic.

I am of course indebted to the very important writings of Professor Edgar A. Singer, Jr., and Professor Henry Bradford Smith. No serious student of Aristotelian logic can fail to be influenced by Professor Singer's *Syllabus of Logic* (published in Professor Smith's *Letters on Logic*, pp. 46–52) nor by Professor Smith's *Primer of Logic, Non-Aristotelian Logic, Letters on Logic, Foundations of Formal Logic, First Book in Logic, System of Formal Logic, Symbolic Logic*, and other writings.

I have endeavoured to acknowledge in the text all points of indebtedness to these authors, but as their influence on the present work is pervasive the detailed acknowledgments are perhaps not complete.

Aside from differences of method and detail, the present work differs from the writings of Professor Singer and Professor Smith as follows: maintaining that the principal issues in Aristotelian logic as it now exists are concerned with the problem of *negative terms*, it aims to be a complete treatment of Aristotelian logic as containing negative terms.

To my friends Professor C. I. Lewis of Harvard University, Mrs. Susanne K. Langer of Radcliffe College, Professor Kurt E. Rosinger of Woman's College of the University of North Carolina, Professor H. S. Leonard of Duke University, Professor Paul Henle of the University of Michigan, and Professor Charles T. Harrison of the College of William and Mary in Virginia, all of whom read the work in its original form and made valuable criticisms, I am under deep obligations. They are of course not responsible for the views expressed in this book nor for any errors which it may contain.

Finally, I wish to express my gratitude to Harvard University for a grant from the Milton Fund for secretarial assistance and to the Department of Philosophy of Harvard University for a subsidy which made publication possible.

July, 1938

1

INTRODUCTION

1. Preliminary Definition of Aristotelian Logic. The most striking features of Aristotelian or traditional[1] logic are the following. First, it is a "subject-predicate" logic and is therefore concerned only with a portion of the sum total of logical truth. It contains, for example, no logic of relations and no logic of unanalysed propositions, but confines itself to the four forms of categorical proposition known as the *A, E, I,* and *O* forms.[2] In the second place, it treats subalternation as a valid form of inference. That is, it assigns (tacitly at least) conventional meanings, different from those employed in modern (*i.e.* symbolic or mathematical) logic, to the four categorical forms, meanings such that subalternation holds.

These two characteristics, however, are not sufficient to define Aristotelian logic. For an indefinite number of systems could be devised which possess these two properties. Since further distinguishing traits of Aristotelian logic will appear only in the course of our investigation, a definition of Aristotelian logic framed in terms of its essential properties cannot be given at the outset.

Nevertheless some preliminary definition of the subject which we intend to study is desirable. One might think that for this purpose a reference to the origin of Aristotelian logic would suffice, and that the most reasonable preliminary definition of Aristotelian logic would be " the system of logic set forth in the logical works of Aristotle." However, Aristotelian logic has developed since the time of its founder. Our subject matter, since our interests in this book are not historical, is traditional logic as it exists at present. (In view of the leisureliness of progress in traditional logic, the "present" will mean roughly the last hundred years.)

---

[1] The expressions " Aristotelian logic " and " traditional logic " are used interchangeably throughout this book.
[2] An appendix entitled " Review of Introductory Aristotelian Logic " is added to this chapter (Sec. 9). In it is defined the usual technical terminology of Aristotelian logic.

Now, traditional logic has been expounded in recent decades principally in introductory manuals of logic. Though differing superficially, these works all possess essentially the same logical content. They all set forth in much the same fashion a certain system of deductive logic which is easily identifiable. It is to that system that one means to refer when one says " traditional logic." As the account of deductive logic given in the leading " introductions to logic " has come to be regarded as the standard exposition of traditional logic, our subject matter may conveniently be defined as the system of deductive logic expounded in the principal introductory textbooks of logic; for example, the well-known manuals by Whately, Jevons, Joseph, Wolf, Creighton, Hibben, and Sellars.[1] This definition is of course a loose one. But I know of none more accurate which could be agreed upon at the outset.[2]

2. Exclusion of Irrelevant Material. Our preliminary definition may seem to be more inclusive than it actually is. We propose to study the deductive *logic* common to the textbooks. But not everything which appears in the textbooks is really logic. The " categories," the " predicables," " classification and division," the " rules of definition," the " enthymeme," " material fallacies," etc., these, following what I take to be the concensus of authoritative opinion, I regard as bits of metaphysics, epistemology, psychology, rhetoric, and grammar, and not parts of logic at all. They therefore do not fall under my definition and shall not be treated in this book.

Further, I exclude from consideration the hypothetical and disjunctive forms of proposition and hypothetical and disjunctive arguments, not indeed on the ground that they are foreign to logic, but because the traditional treatment of them is very fragmentary and is not distinctive, and because an adequate account of them would take us far beyond the intended scope of

---

[1] R. Whately: *Elements of Logic*. W. S. Jevons: *Elementary Lessons in Logic*. H. W. B. Joseph: *An Introduction to Logic*. A. Wolf: *Essentials of Logic*; and *Textbook of Logic*. J. E. Creighton: *An Introductory Logic*. J. G. Hibben: *Logic: Deductive and Inductive*. R. W. Sellars: *The Essentials of Logic*.

[2] The appendix at the end of this chapter will serve to make the definition fully explicit.

traditional logic and would coincide with the modern calculus of propositional functions.

What remains, then, is immediate inference (including both eduction and the square of opposition), the syllogism, and the sorites; in short, the traditional categorical forms of proposition and the traditional forms of argument the premises and conclusion of which are all categorical.

3. **The Aim of this Book.** Traditional logic, in the present stage of its development, differs from its earlier forms in one major respect. Traditional logic as it now exists is a system which contains negative terms (as in obversion, contraposition, etc.), whereas, prior to the nineteenth century, negative terms had not been admitted.

The inclusion of negative terms in traditional logic ought to have resulted in a great logical simplification of the system. Instead it led to nothing but confusion and contradiction. For unfortunately the standard expositors of traditional logic, namely, the authors of the manuals of logic, failed to be aware that the addition of negative terms necessitated drastic changes in the system.

The aim of the present book is to effect the reorganizations which are required by the presence of negative terms in the system, and, at the same time, to give a rigorous presentation of traditional logic as containing negative terms.

4. **The Problems of this Book.** This book may be divided into three parts. The first, which consists of Chapters I–IV, solves the problem of the *systematization* of traditional logic. The second, consisting of Chapters V–VI, solves the problem of the *rules* of traditional logic. And the third, consisting of Chapter VII, solves the problem of the *interpretation* of traditional logic. The solution of these three problems effects the changes that are required by the presence of negative terms in the system, and constitutes a complete presentation of traditional logic.

In the next three sections these problems are stated.

5. **The Problem of Systematization.** Our first task consists in expounding what forms of argument are valid, in traditional logic, and what forms are invalid.

This exposition, however, cannot consist in a mere enumeration, for the forms of argument are infinite. Nor is a mere enumeration systematic. The postulational method accordingly recommends itself.

We shall proceed then as follows. We shall set down certain undefined ideas (or symbols) in terms of which all the other ideas (or symbols) which appear in the system of traditional logic may be defined, and certain assumed propositions or postulates from which all the other principles of the system may be deduced. Then we shall deduce important theorems, and finally shall show that all the principles of traditional logic either have been assumed or deduced or can be deduced.

This application of the postulational method to traditional logic, one should note, merely carries to its completion an undertaking which Aristotle himself began. Aristotle used precisely this method, but applied it only to the valid forms of the syllogism. We shall treat the whole of traditional logic by this method, deducing forms of immediate inference and sorites as well as of syllogism, deducing forms which involve negative terms as well as those which do not, and deducing the invalidity of invalid forms as well as the validity of valid ones.

To the solution of this problem we shall devote Chapters I to IV inclusive. In Chapter I we shall deal with various preliminary matters and then give our assumed ideas, postulates, and definitions. In Chapter II we shall deduce the forms of immediate inference; and in Chapter III, the forms of syllogism and sorites. Chapter IV will be concerned with certain special matters, the treatment of which is necessary for the ideal completion of our system and which will require the introduction of one further postulate.

6. The Problem of the Rules. Traditional logic includes sets of rules for various forms of inference or argument. These rules serve many purposes. By means of them one may test given arguments for validity. They are of aid in finding what conclusions follow from a given premise or given premises, and in finding from what premise or premises a given conclusion may be deduced.

Before the introduction of negative terms into traditional logic, sets of rules for the principal forms of argument had been devised. Thus rules for eduction (usually called " rules for conversion ") and rules for the syllogism were part of the tradition. General rules for the sorites were not ordinarily stated, but could easily be constructed by extending the rules for the syllogism in obvious ways. These sets of rules constituted necessary and sufficient conditions for the validity of the forms of argument to which they applied. They were formulated in terms of distribution, quantity, and quality, and were consistent with everything in traditional logic.

With the introduction of negative terms into the system, however, these sets of rules became antiquated, though the manuals continued to state and use them unchanged. The presence of negative terms in the system requires that the rules be revised for the following two reasons.

In the first place, negative terms give rise to a contradiction, or at least to the appearance of one, in traditional logic. This may be seen by considering, for example, the following forms of argument : (1) *All s is p therefore No s is non-p.* (2) *All s is p therefore All non-p is non-s.* (3) *All s is p therefore Some non-s is not p.* (4) *All s is m and All m is p therefore All non-p is non-s.* Now all of these forms of argument are admittedly valid in traditional logic. But, as the doctrine of distribution is ordinarily understood, they all distribute a term in the conclusion which is not distributed in a premise and thus violate a general rule of inference. Now this contradiction never arises except in the case of arguments that involve negative terms. In order to accommodate negative terms, therefore, a new treatment of distribution is needed.

Second, when negative terms have been admitted, the old sets of rules are no longer complete. The old rules for eduction do not apply to eductions involving negative terms : a set of rules is required which will apply to all forms of eduction whether they involve negative terms or not. In the case of the syllogism, the definition of syllogism ought obviously to be extended to cover such arguments as *All m is p and All s is m therefore All non-p is non-s ;* and, as the old rules for the syllogism do not apply to such forms of argument, a new set of rules is demanded. Similarly, rules for the sorites should be given which will hold whether or not negative terms are involved.

Chapters V and VI will deal with the rules. We shall remove the contradiction and provide sets of rules for all the species of arguments in traditional logic.

7. The Problem of Interpretation. In our treatment of the foregoing two problems our point of view will be entirely abstract. We shall not as yet inquire into the meaning of the four propositional forms with which we deal. *All*, *No*, *Some*, *is*, and *is not* will be left quite indeterminate. Similarly with s and p: whether they stand for classes or concepts or something else will not be inquired. The A, E, I, and O propositions will be taken merely as so many counters, which " move " in certain prescribed ways in the game of traditional logic.

But in Chapter VII we shall abandon our abstract point of view and shall ask what precise meaning, what interpretation, is to be given to *All s is p* and the other propositional forms.

This question is liable to a misunderstanding. One might suppose that we are asking what is the " real " meaning of *All s is p*, that we are searching for a predetermined meaning which belongs by right to *All s is p* and which must be assigned to *All s is p* in every system of logic. Surely a little reflection will convince one that such an inquiry would be illegitimate. There is no uniquely proper significance affixed to the expression *All s is p* by the nature of things. Neither does *All s is p* possess in ordinary discourse a perfectly clear and invariable meaning; ordinary speech is neither explicit nor consistent in its intentions concerning " existential import." The logician is free to interpret *All s is p* as he sees fit, provided of course that he does not select a meaning too remote from common usage. Moreover the interpretation adopted in one system of logic (for example, traditional logic) need not be the same as that adopted in another (for example, the Boolean logic of classes). It is all a matter of convention.

Our problem accordingly is simply this : to find an interpretation of *All s is p* and the other forms which approximates to ordinary usage and which satisfies our postulates.

This problem, though capable of a simple and precise solution, has ordinarily been neglected by the traditional manuals of logic. On the other hand solutions have been proposed and have gained some acceptance which nevertheless fail at crucial points. For example, it is sometimes supposed, I believe, that traditional logic will be validated if one takes s and p to stand for classes and allows the A form to mean "s is included in p and there is s," the E form "s is included in $non\text{-}p$ and there is s," the I form "there is s which is p," and the O form "there is s which is $non\text{-}p$." But on this interpretation several principles of traditional logic would fail to hold: for example, the E proposition would not be simply convertible, the A proposition would not imply its full contrapositive, and neither A and O nor E and I would be contradictories.

The only writers, so far as I am aware, who have treated the problem of interpretation satisfactorily are Professor E. A. Singer, Jr., and Professor H. B. Smith. They have proposed interpretations of the A, E, I, and O forms which satisfy all of the principles of traditional logic except those which involve negative terms.[1] And finally Professor Smith[2] has given a most ingenious interpretation which satisfies all of the principles of traditional logic including those which involve negative terms.

The contribution of this book to the problem of interpretation will consist in the proposal of two further interpretations which satisfy all the principles of traditional logic including those which involve negative terms and which possess certain advantages over Professor Smith's interpretation.

8. General Conclusions. The solution of our three problems will enable us to answer certain general questions about the nature of traditional logic. Two such questions are these: is traditional logic a correct system of logic, that is to say, is it genuinely a part of logic? and what are the relations of Aristotelian logic to modern (*i.e.* symbolic) logic? As a result of

---

[1] E. A. Singer, Jr.: *Syllabus of Logic* (in H. B. Smith's *Letters on Logic*, p. 53). H. B. Smith: *Foundations of Formal Logic*, p. 54; *A First Book in Logic*, p. 168.
[2] H. B. Smith: *A System of Formal Logic*, p. 47; *Symbolic Logic*, p. 61.

our treatment of the three problems we shall be able to show that traditional logic is a correct though limited system of logic, and that, in spite of appearances to the contrary, traditional and modern logic are in perfect agreement, that in fact traditional logic is a part of or a special case of the wider and more general system envisaged in modern logic.

9. Appendix. Review of Introductory Aristotelian Logic.
In order to make our preliminary definition of traditional logic as explicit as possible, as well as for purposes of reference, the following brief review of introductory traditional logic is given. It includes only the essentials, and aims to be a sort of composite picture, on a greatly reduced scale, of the standard manuals of logic.

(a) The propositional forms

Four kinds of proposition are recognized: namely, *All s is p*, *No s is p*, *Some s is p*, and *Some s is not p*.

They are called the *A*, *E*, *I*, and *O* forms, respectively.

The *A* and *E* forms are said to be *universal;* the *I* and *O* forms, *particular*. The *A* and *I* forms are called *affirmative;* the *E* and *O*, *negative*. The distinction between universal and particular is called a distinction of *quantity;* that between affirmative and negative, one of *quality*.

In each of these forms four constituents may be noted. First is the subject; it is that about which something is asserted; we have written these forms in such a way that the subject is symbolized in each case by *s*, though of course any other letter would do as well. Second is the *predicate;* it is that which is asserted of the subject; it is indicated above by *p*. The subject and predicate of a proposition are called its *terms*. Third is the *copula*, the word " is," which states the connection between the subject and the predicate. Fourth is the *quantifier* (though it would be more accurate to call it " the quantifier and qualifier "); the quantifier in the *A* form is *All;* in the *E* form, *No;* in the *I* form, *Some;* in the *O* form, *Some . . . not*.

The following abbreviations may be used to symbolize the *A*, *E*, *I*, and *O* forms, respectively: *sAp*, *sEp*, *sIp*, and *sOp*.

(b) *Immediate and mediate inference*

When one proposition is inferred (*i.e.* deduced) from another or from others, the proposition which is inferred is called the *conclusion*, the proposition or propositions from which the inference is made is called the *premise* or *premises*. When there is but one premise, the inference is called *immediate*. When there are two or more premises, the inference is called *mediate*.

Two kinds of immediate inference may be distinguished: *eduction* and *opposition*. The two kinds of mediate inference are *syllogism* and *sorites*.

(c) *Eduction*

The meaning of *eduction* will be made sufficiently clear by the following enumeration of the species of eduction.

Simple conversion is the process of transposing the subject and predicate of a proposition, the quantity and quality remaining the same. The simple conversion of E and I propositions is valid; that is, from an E or an I proposition the simple converse may be legitimately inferred; but the simple conversion of A and O propositions is invalid.[1]

Conversion by limitation (or *per accidens*). Conversion by limitation is the process of transposing the subject and predicate of a universal proposition, and of changing the quantity from universal to particular, the quality remaining the same. Conversion by limitation of A and of E propositions is valid.

Obversion (or *Permutation* or *Immediate Inference by Privative Conception*, etc., as it is variously called) is the process of negating (contradicting) the predicate and changing the quality of the proposition, the subject and the quantity of the proposition remaining the same. For example, the obverse of *All s is p* is *No s is non-p*. Any proposition may be validly obverted.[2]

---

[1] Whether we define simple conversion in such a way that A and O propositions have *no* simple converse, or in such a way that they have simple converses though the process of simply converting is invalid, is a matter of indifference. Some writers prefer one alternative, some the other. We have adopted the latter alternative.

[2] Obversion is especially important because it introduces negative terms (i.e. contradictory terms) into the system of traditional logic. By " negative terms " are meant such terms as *non-s*, *non-p*, etc. For every term *s*, there is a negative term *non-s*. A term is so related to its negative that on the one hand they are mutually exclusive, and on the other hand they are jointly exhaustive of the entire universe; nothing can be both *s* and *non-s*, everything must be either *s* or *non-s*.

Compound forms of eduction. Successive applications of the foregoing three kinds of eduction give rise to various compound forms, certain of which have been called *contraposition* and *inversion.*

(d) Opposition

Two propositions are said to be *opposed* when the subject of one is the same as the subject of the other and the predicate of one is the same as the predicate of the other.

The various relations which may hold between opposed propositions are indicated by the notions of " contradiction," " contrariety," " subcontrariety," and " subalternation."

Two opposed propositions are said to be mutually *contradictory* when from the truth of one the falsity of the other follows and when from the falsity of one the truth of the other follows. A and O are mutually contradictory, as are also E and I; (it is of course understood that we are speaking of propositions which have the same subject and the same predicate).

Two opposed propositions are said to be mutually *contrary* when from the truth of one the falsity of the other follows and when from the falsity of one nothing follows about the truth or falsity of the other. A and E are mutually contrary.

Two opposed propositions are said to be mutually *subcontrary* when from the falsity of one the truth of the other follows and when from the truth of one nothing follows about the truth or falsity of the other. I and O are mutually subcontrary.

A proposition is said to be the subaltern of an opposed proposition when from the truth of the latter the truth of the former follows and when from the falsity of the latter nothing follows about the truth or falsity of the former. I is the subaltern of A; and O, of E.

(e) Distribution

Before we proceed further it will be convenient to introduce the notion of *distribution*, which plays an important part in the *rules* for various kinds of inference.

Definition of distribution. A term is said to be *distributed* by a proposition when the proposition states or implies something about *all* of the term.

From the above definition the following *table of distribution* may be derived. The table is an exhaustive list of the terms which are distributed by the *A*, *E*, *I*, and *O* propositions respectively.

A : subject;
E : subject and predicate;
O : predicate.

The importance of the notion of distribution is largely due to what we may call *the principle of distribution* : no term may be distributed in the conclusion of any inference which is not distributed in a premise.

(*f*) *Rules for conversion*

By means of the concept of distribution, aided by the notion of quality, we may now give a set of rules for conversion (whether simple or by limitation) :

1. If the premise is affirmative, the conclusion must be affirmative.

2. If the premise is negative, the conclusion must be negative.

3. If a term is distributed in the conclusion, it must be distributed in the premise.

These rules are necessary and sufficient conditions for valid conversion. If conversion is performed in accordance with them it is valid; if not, invalid.[1]

(*g*) *Syllogism : definitions*

A *syllogism* is an argument with two premises and a conclusion, where a term of one premise is the same as a term of the other premise, and where the other two terms of the premises are the same as the terms of the conclusion.

The *middle term* is the term which is common to the premises. The *minor term* is the term which is the subject of the conclusion. The *major term* is the term which is the predicate of the conclusion. The *minor premise* is the premise which contains the minor term. The *major premise* is the premise which contains the major term.

---

[1] These rules have a wider significance than the title " rules for conversion " indicates. As a matter of fact, they are rules for *eduction* in what we may call the " System of Traditional Logic without Negative Terms "; that is to say, when we mean by eduction all forms of immediate inference where the subject and predicate of the conclusion are the same respectively as the subject and predicate of the premise or the predicate and subject of the premise, these rules are necessary and sufficient conditions of the validity of eduction.

(h) The syllogistic figures

By the *figure* of a syllogism is meant the arrangement of the terms in a syllogism.

A syllogism is said to be in the *first figure* when the middle term is the subject of the major premise and the predicate of the minor premise. It is said to be in the *second figure* when the middle term is the predicate of both premises. It is said to be in the *third figure* when the middle term is the subject of both premises. It is said to be in the *fourth figure* when the middle term is the predicate of the major premise and the subject of the minor premise. The following diagrams, in which the first line stands for the major premise, the second line for the minor premise, and the third line for the conclusion, are helpful.

First Figure	Second Figure	Third Figure	Fourth Figure
m p	p m	m p	p m
s m	s m	m s	m s
s p	s p	s p	s p

(i) The valid moods of the syllogism

In each figure there are sixty-four arithmetically possible forms (or *moods*) of syllogism; for the major premise may be either an *A*, *E*, *I*, or *O* proposition, and similarly with the minor premise and conclusion. Thus there are altogether two hundred and fifty-six arithmetically possible forms (or moods) of syllogism. But only some of these moods are valid.

The following abbreviation is useful in referring to a given syllogistic mood. For example, "*EIO* in the first figure" will mean that form of syllogism in which the major premise is an *E* proposition, the minor premise an *I*, and the conclusion an *O*, and which is in the first figure.

The following is the complete list of the *valid* syllogistic moods.

First figure: *AAA, EAE, AII, EIO, AAI, EAO.*
Second figure: *EAE, AEE, EIO, AOO, EAO, AEO.*
Third figure: *AAI, IAI, AII, EAO, OAO, EIO.*
Fourth figure: *AAI, AEE, IAI, EAO, EIO, AEE.*

Thus, of the two hundred and fifty-six arithmetically possible moods, twenty-four are valid (six in each figure) and the rest are invalid.

The valid moods are often referred to by the following names. (Those in parentheses I have added for the sake of completeness.)

First figure : *Barbara, Celarent, Darii, Ferio, (Weakened Barbara), (Weakened Celarent).*

Second figure : *Cesare, Camestres, Festino, Baroko, (Weakened Cesare), (Weakened Camestres).*

Third figure : *Darapti, Disamis, Datisi, Felapton, Bokardo, Ferison.*

Fourth figure : *Bramantip, Camenes, Dimaris, Fesapo, Fresison, (Weakened Camenes).*

The valid syllogistic moods are indicated by the vowels in these names. Thus *Ferio* means the mood *EIO* (in the first figure).

(j) *The syllogistic rules*

The following are the *rules* of the syllogism (*i.e.* necessary and sufficient conditions of validity for any syllogism).

1. If the middle term is undistributed in a premise, it must be distributed in the other premise. (A violation of this rule is called a "fallacy of undistributed middle.")

2. If a term is distributed in the conclusion, it must be distributed in a premise. (A violation of this rule is called a "fallacy of the illicit process.")

3. If a premise is negative, the other must be affirmative.

4. If a premise is negative, the conclusion must be negative.

5. If the conclusion is negative, a premise must be negative.

From these rules two corollaries follow :

1. If a premise is particular, the other premise must be universal.

2. If a premise is particular, the conclusion must be particular.

These corollaries are of course necessary conditions of validity. But they need not be included explicitly in our list of rules since they are already included implicitly (*i.e.* are deducible from the five rules).

(k) *Sorites*

By a *sorites* is meant an argument consisting of a chain of syllogisms all the conclusions of which, with the exception of the last, are suppressed.

Two kinds of sorites are recognized : the *Aristotelian* and the *Goclenian*. An Aristotelian sorites is one in which the minor premise comes first; *e.g., All a is b, All b is c, and All c is d, therefore All a is d*. A Goclenian sorites is one in which the major premise comes first; *e.g., All c is d, All b is c, and All a is b, therefore All a is d*.

The textbooks give no general set of rules for the sorites. Instead they provide merely special rules for the two species of sorites just mentioned.

The special rules[1] for the Aristotelian sorites are:
NOTE—

1. If a premise is negative, it must be the last, and the other premises must be affirmative.

2. If a premise is particular, it must be the first, and the other premises must be universal.

The special rules for the Goclenian sorites are the same except that the words "first" and "last" are interchanged.

---

[1] Whether these rules are sufficient, as well as necessary, conditions of validity for the Aristotelian sorites is not ordinarily stated. As a matter of fact they are not sufficient conditions of validity. Similarly with the special rules for the Goclenian sorites.

CHAPTER I

POSTULATES FOR ARISTOTELIAN LOGIC[1]

The task of the first four chapters is to formulate traditional logic as a deductive system. The present chapter will lay the foundation for this systematization; that is, it will give the undefined ideas, the postulates, and the definitions of the system.

We must begin with two preliminary matters, however. First, it will be instructive to note the partial systematization which appears in the introductory manuals of logic. Second, we must consider the general character which our systematization will have.

10. Reduction as Deduction. The standard textbooks of logic, following the procedure of Aristotle himself, give a partial systematization of traditional logic. This appears in the customary chapters on " the reduction of the imperfect figures of the syllogism." A close scrutiny of " reduction " will show that it is nothing more nor less than an incomplete application of the postulational method to Aristotelian logic. *Reduction* of one form of syllogism *to* another, is the same as *deduction* of the former *from* the latter. In the textbooks all of the valid forms of syllogism in the second, third, and fourth figures are " reduced " to the valid forms in the first figure ; that is simply another way of stating that from the valid forms of the first figure the other valid forms are *deduced*. In short, the textbooks take the valid forms of the first figure as axioms or postulates, and from them deduce the others as theorems.

[1] Sets of postulates for traditional logic and analogous systems have been given previously by Professor E. A. Singer, Jr., and Professor H. B. Smith. The present set differs from theirs not only in method and detail, but also in the fact that while negative terms are elements in the present system we do not introduce forms of proposition other than the A, E, I, and O. Thus in Professor Singer's system presented in his *Syllabus of Logic* and in the sets of postulates given by Professor Smith in his *Letters on Logic* and in his *First Book in Logic* negative terms are not elements of the system. On the other hand in Professor Smith's sets of postulates in his *Primer of Logic, Non-Aristotelian Logic, Foundations of Formal Logic, System of Formal Logic,* and *Symbolic Logic* the basic forms are the α, β, γ, and ϵ forms, which involve quantification of the predicate.

This matter of reduction may be carried even further, as some of the textbooks suggest. For we need not postulate all six valid forms of the first figure. The weakened forms of *Barbara* and *Celarent* may be reduced "directly" to *Barbara* and *Celarent* themselves. Also, *Darii* and *Ferio* may be reduced "indirectly" to *Celarent*. *Barbara* and *Celarent* are thus sufficient to yield all the other forms, as Aristotle himself was aware; and this is what is meant by saying that the whole theory of the syllogism is covered by the *dictum de omni et nullo*. Finally, by means of obversion, *Celarent* may be reduced directly to *Barbara*. Therefore, from *Barbara* all of the other twenty-three valid forms of the syllogism may be deduced, our list of postulates is cut down to one, and the whole theory of the syllogism is covered by the *dictum de omni*.

Certain misapprehensions about the nature of this reduction of all forms of valid syllogisms to *Barbara* need to be guarded against.

In the first place, it might be assumed that *Barbara* acquires a certain priority or preëminence as a result of this reduction. In one sense this is true; in that particular systematization *Barbara* is prior to the others. But *Barbara* need not be made prior. Other syllogistic forms will serve quite as well. With the exception of the forms which have both premises universal but the conclusion particular, *any one* of the valid forms may replace *Barbara* as postulate. There are accordingly sixteen syllogistic forms from any one of which all the valid forms may be deduced. Another reason why *Barbara*—and the other syllogisms of the first figure—are supposed to be preëminent is that they are held to be more "natural" and "self-evident" than syllogisms in the other figures. This, however, is an epistemological or perhaps psychological matter, and need not concern us.

Another misapprehension to be noted is the supposition that the *dictum de omni et nullo* is more fundamental than *Barbara* and *Celarent* themselves. The dictum may be taken in either of two ways. First, it may be regarded as merely stating in verbal form what *Barbara* and *Celarent* state in quasi-symbolic form; in that case it is just the same thing in a different medium of expression, and can claim no greater profundity. Second, it may be considered as the *interpretation* of the abstract forms *Barbara* and *Celarent*; but how an interpretation can be considered deductively more fundamental than the abstract system to which it applies is not clear.

A third misapprehension would be the supposition that because only one form of the *syllogism* need be assumed, nothing *else* need be assumed in order to deduce all of the valid forms of the syllogism. Now the deduction of the other valid syllogisms from *Barbara*—or from any other postulated syllogistic form—makes use of simple conversion, conversion by limitation, the relation of contradiction on the square of opposition, and obversion. Unless these principles of eduction and opposition could all be deduced from our syllogistic axiom—and they cannot—further assumptions are required. In affirming that *Barbara* yields all the other forms of the syllogism we intend the tacit proviso " on certain assumptions about immediate inference and opposition."

The ordinary presentation of traditional logic thus employs the postulational method, but the resulting systematization is a partial one only. It is incomplete in the following respects.

First, a system ought to state what its undefined or primitive ideas are and ought to define all the other ideas of the system in terms of these primitive ones. To lay down postulates and derive theorems is not sufficient. The ideas of the system should also be set forth, some as assumed and some as defined. But the systematization given in the textbooks is entirely lacking in this respect.

Second, not only the forms of the syllogism but also the forms of eduction and the principles of the square of opposition ought to be systematized. They are part of traditional logic; moreover, they are required for the deduction of the forms of the syllogism. Each one of them should appear either as a postulate or as a theorem. Here also the ordinary account of traditional logic is defective.

Third, the textbooks fail to treat postulationally the principles of invalidity. By a principle of invalidity I mean, for example, such a proposition as *It is false that for all values of s, m, and p, All m is p* and *All m is s* implies *All s is p*. In a complete systematization of traditional logic that proposition would appear either as a postulate or as a theorem.

11. General Character of our Systematization. But one further preliminary need detain us. Before we begin the task of systematizing traditional logic, we must consider the general character which our systematization is to have.

We propose to formulate traditional logic as a deductive system. But there are two species of deductive systems, and we must explain to which species our system belongs.[1]

One type of deductive system may be called the *logistic* type. The distinguishing feature of that kind of system is the fact that the general principles of logic, by means of which the theorems are deduced from the postulates, are themselves contained in the postulates of the system, and that the general ideas of logic, by means of which the postulates, definitions, and theorems are stated, are themselves assumed ideas of the system or are definable in terms of the assumed ideas without the use of any further ideas. Examples of this kind of system are (1) Whitehead and Russell's system of logic set forth in their *Principia Mathematica* and (2) C. I. Lewis's "System of Strict Implication."

The other and more common type of system may be called *non-logistic*. In this type of system, though the theorems are deduced rigorously from the postulates, this deduction is effected by means of general principles of logic which are not themselves contained in the postulates. These principles are *outside* the system, so to speak. By means of these principles which are external to the system, the system is generated. Moreover, in systems of this type, certain ideas of logic, which are not part of the system itself, are employed to state the posutlates, definitions, and theorems of the system. Most of the modern "sets of postulates" are of this sort; for example, Professor Huntington's sets of postulates for Boolean algebra (the modern logic of classes), and his postulates for geometry.

Now our system will be of the second rather than the first type; it will be *non-logistic*. Indeed it must be so. For the logistic

---

[1] Cf. C. I. Lewis: *Survey of Symbolic Logic*, p. 324.

method can be used only in the case of a subject matter of a peculiarly fundamental nature. The fact that we shall thus use principles and ideas of logic which are outside our system is not a logical defect; it is simply a characteristic which belongs inevitably to many systems.

The ideas of logic which are not part of the system but which we shall use to state our postulates, definitions, and theorems are the following : " implication," " equivalence," " negation," and " conjunction." When we say that one proposition, p, "implies" another, q, we mean that if p is true then q is true.[1] To say that p " is equivalent to " q means that p and q mutually imply each other. The notion of negation, expressed by the words " is false," is used in the ordinary sense and is so simple that any explanation is at once difficult and, in this work, unnecessary. Similarly, conjunction, expressed by the word " and," requires no explanation. The words " implication," " equivalence," etc., might conveniently be replaced, throughout our systematization, by ideographic symbols of the sort that are commonly used in mathematical logic ; but, in order to stress the fact that the ideas which these words express are *not part of the system*, I shall adhere to the use of the words.

The main principles of logic which we shall use to deduce our theorems are the following (where p, q, and r stand for any propositions) :

1. (p and q) is equivalent to (q and p).
2. If p implies q and if p implies r, then p implies q and r.
3. If p implies q and if q implies r, then p implies r.
4. (p implies q) is equivalent to (q-is-false implies p-is-false).
5. [(p and q) implies r] is equivalent to [(p and r-is-false) implies q-is-false].
6. (p is equivalent to q) is equivalent to (q is equivalent to p).
7. (p is equivalent to q) is equivalent to (q-is-false is equivalent to p-is-false).
8. If p is equivalent to q and if q is equivalent to r, then p is equivalent to r.

---

[1] Students of contemporary issues in logic will perhaps demand a more explicit characterization of " implication." " Implication " may be taken throughout this book as either *material* or *strict*, whichever the reader prefers, provided that he adhere consistently to the same meaning throughout.

12. Primitive Ideas. We are now ready to begin our systematization of traditional logic. The first step is to state the assumed or primitive ideas of the system. They are as follows :

1. The idea of the elements of the system, which are symbolized by small letters of the alphabet. (We shall follow the custom of traditional logicians and use s, p, and m, rather than a, b, and c.)
2. The idea symbolized by sEp.
3. The idea symbolized by s'.

13. Discussion of the Primitive Ideas. These ideas may be thought of entirely abstractly. Or, if one prefers, one may relax the rigors of complete formalism and think of these symbols as having the following meanings :

1. s, p, m, etc., may be taken to stand for the *terms* of traditional categorical propositions.
2. sEp may be regarded as representing the traditional E form of proposition and may be read *No s is p*. The assumption of sAp rather than sEp as an undefined idea would perhaps seem more natural ; but in the sequel we shall see that sEp is the more convenient assumption.
3. s' may be read *non-s*, and accordingly may be considered as symbolizing the term which is the contradictory or negative of the term s.

These readings, however, are quasi-abstract. For we cannot as yet say what is meant by " the terms of traditional categorical propositions," nor what is meant by *No s is p*. Whether the terms are classes, or concepts, or something else ; whether *No s is p* has " existential import " or not, and if so what kind : these are difficult questions, the answers to which must be deferred to Chapter VII. The readings accordingly amount to little more than indications of the regions in which we shall later search for a meaning to assign to our abstract system.

14. Postulates of Validity. The following are our postulates of validity, that is, postulates from which the valid forms of argument may be deduced. For convenience of reference they are assigned decimal numbers. *They are assumed to hold for all elements of the system.*

1.1   If s is an element, s' is an element
1.2 sEp is equivalent to sEp''
1.3 sEp implies $s'Ep$ is false
1.4 sEm' and pEm implies sEp
1.5 sEp implies pEp'

15. Discussion of the Postulates of Validity. Postulates 1.2–1.5 are ambiguous, as they stand, because of the omission of brackets. These postulates are to be understood as having the following meanings. Postulate 1.2 : $\{s\,E\,p\}$ is equivalent to $\{[s]\,E\,[(p')']\}$. Postulate 1.3 : $\{s\,E\,p\}$ implies $\{[(s')\,E\,(p)]$ is false$\}$. Postulate 1.4 : $\{[(s)\,E\,(m')]$ and $[pEm]\}$ implies $\{sEp\}$. Postulate 1.5 : $[sEp]$ implies $[(p)\,E\,(p')]$. We hereby adopt conventions such that brackets may be omitted with these meanings.

Postulate 1.1 states that every term has a contradictory or negative term. In virtue of this postulate we may replace a term by its negative in any postulate, definition, or theorem, provided such substitution is complete. For example, we may write p' for p in 1.4, and thus may assert the proposition : sEm' and $p'Em$ implies sEp'. But we would not be justified in asserting : sEm' and $p'Em$ implies sEp. For here the substitution is not complete ; *i.e.* we have written p' for p in pEm but have not done so in sEp.

Postulate 1.2 may be read *No s is p is equivalent to No s is non-non-p*. It is a principle of double negation.

Postulate 1.3, as we shall see later, is equivalent to the principle of subalternation. It may be regarded as the distinctive postulate of the system.

Postulate 1.4, in virtue of Definition 1.91 (Sec. 19), is equivalent to *Cesare*. The postulation of a syllogistic form of the first figure might seem more natural ; but *Cesare* happens to be more powerful, deductively, than any of the " perfect moods." In this postulate and in the syllogistic theorems I take the liberty of reversing the procedure of the textbooks of traditional logic and write the minor premise first, for reasons of convenience.

Postulate 1.5 is an unfamiliar principle, the justification for the inclusion of which in a systematization of traditional logic is that every interpretation which can be supposed to represent the intended meaning of traditional logic satisfies this postulate. (See Chapter VII.)

16. Postulate of Invalidity. From the following postulate the invalidity of the invalid forms may be deduced. It is hence called a postulate of invalidity.

1.6   There exist elements s, m, and p, such that sEm and mEp and sEp.

17. Discussion of the Postulate of Invalidity. The distinctness of s, m, and p need not be specified, for it is deducible.

The reader who is averse to complete abstractness and who wishes to anticipate the results of Chapter VII may " verify " this postulate by an example. Thus, letting s stand, say, for " infants," m for " adolescents," and p for " adults," one sees that this postulate holds for traditional logic.

18. Note on the Postulates. For the ideal completion of our system one further postulate is required. It will be introduced in Chapter IV.

19. Definitions.

1.91 $sAp = sEp'$ Definition
1.92 $sIp\ = sEp$ is false   Definition
1.93 $sOp = sAp$ is false   Definition

20. Discussion of the Definitions. sAp, sIp, and sOp may be read *All s is p*, *Some s is p*, and *Some s is not p* respectively. sAp is defined in terms of its " obverse." sIp and sOp are defined in terms of the doctrine of " contradiction " on the " square of opposition."

21. Functions. In order to give precise definitions of eduction, syllogism, and other species of argument, the following symbols[1] are introduced.

sXp is a function the values of which are sAp, sEp, sIp, and sOp.

---

[1] These symbols are similar to certain ones employed by Professor E. A. Singer, Jr., and Professor H. B. Smith.

$X(s,p)$ is a function the values of which are sAp, sEp, sIp, sOp, pAs, pEs, pIs, and pOs.

sYp is a function the values of which are all of the A, E, I, and O propositions the subject of which is s or s' and the predicate of which is p or p'.

$Y(s,p)$ is a function the values of which are all of the A, E, I, and O propositions the subject of which is s or s' and the predicate of which is p or p' and all of the A, E, I, and O propositions the subject of which is p or p' and the predicate of which is s or s'.

sZp is a function the values of which are all of the values of sYp and all of the values of sYp *is false*.

$Z(s,p)$ is a function the values of which are all of the values of $Y(s,p)$ and all of the values of $Y(s,p)$ *is false*.

CHAPTER II

IMMEDIATE INFERENCE

22. The Manner of Writing the Proofs. Before we deduce any of our theorems, the manner in which the proofs are written should be explained.

The theorem which is to be proved is first set down. To each theorem will be prefixed a decimal number for purposes of reference. The statement of the theorem is followed immediately by the demonstration. Various steps in the proof are numbered (1), (2), (3), etc., in order that we may refer back to them; such a number, enclosed in parentheses, stands at the extreme right of a step in the proof. The numbers enclosed in brackets at the extreme left of a step in the proof indicate the postulates, definitions, previously proved theorems, or previous steps in the proof, which justify us in asserting the present step in the proof. The notation consisting of two symbols (indicating elements of the system) separated by a slanting bar means that the symbol at the left is to be substituted for the symbol at the right throughout the given step in the proof; thus, p'/s means that p' is to be written for s throughout the step. The last step in the proof is of course the theorem itself; instead of writing it out in full we shall write merely the word " theorem."

23. Substitution. In treating eduction, syllogism, sorites, etc., our usual procedure will be to deduce first a few fundamental theorems and then to point out that all the remaining ones of the species in question can be derived immediately by *substitution* from these fundamental theorems. In order to make this procedure possible we must first explain and justify the principles of substitution. Now there are two kinds of substitution which we shall use: *term substitution* and *propositional substitution*. By *term substitution* is meant the substituting of one element for another throughout a given postulate or previously proved theorem; thus we may write s' for s, or p for s and s for p, etc. By *propositional substitution* is meant the substituting of a propositional form for another *which is equivalent to it*. Term substitution is immediately justified by the postulates.[1] Propositional substitution is justified by the meaning of equivalence. It remains to show what propositional forms are equivalent to what other ones. A theorem which states such a relation of equivalence we shall call a "principle of equivalence." Three kinds of principles of equivalence may be distinguished in traditional logic: principles of eductive equivalence, principles of double negation, and principles of contradiction.

24. The Principles of Eductive Equivalence. By a principle of eductive equivalence is meant a proposition of the form[2]

$$Y_1(s,p) \text{ is equivalent to } Y_2(s,p).$$

We begin by pointing out the forms to which *sEp* is eductively equivalent.

2.11   *sEp* is equivalent to *sEp*

This follows from the meaning of equivalence.

2.11 is a very trivial theorem, which, of course, is of no use in effecting substitution, but which will be required in the sequel.

2.12   *sEp* is equivalent to *pEs*
[1.5, *s/p,p/s*]	*pEs* implies *sEs'*	(1)
[2.11,*s/p,p/s*]	*pEs* implies *pEs*	(2)
[(1);(2)]	*pEs* implies *sEs'* and *pEs*	(3)
[1.4,*s/m*]	*sEs'* and *pEs* implies *sEp*	(4)
[(3);(4)]	*pEs* implies *sEp*	(5)
[(5),*s/p,p/s*]	*sEp* implies *pEs*	(6)
[(5);(6)]	theorem	

2.13   *sEp* is equivalent to *sAp'*
[1.2]	*sEp* is equivalent to *sEp''*	(1)
[(1);1.91]	theorem	

2.14   *sEp* is equivalent to *pAs'*
[2.12]	*sEp* is equivalent to *pEs*	(1)
[2.13,*s/p,p/s*]	*pEs* is equivalent to *pAs'*	(2)
[(1);(2)]	theorem	

---
[1] In the case of principles of *validity*, this follows immediately from the fact that the postulates have been expressly assumed to hold for *all* elements and from postulate 1.1 which states that if *s* is an element, *s'* is an element. Term substitution in principles of invalidity will be justified later (Sec. 31).

[2] For the explanation of the symbols used in this definition see Sec. 21.

Corresponding theorems about sIp follow.

2.15 sIp is equivalent to sIp
This follows from the meaning of equivalence.

2.16 sIp is equivalent to pIs
[2.12] sEp is equivalent to pEs (1)
[(1)] sEp is false is equivalent to pEs is false   (2)
[(2);1.92]   theorem

2.17 sIp is equivalent to sOp'
                 Similarly [2.13;1.92;1.93]

2.18 sIp is equivalent to pOs'
                 Similarly [2.14;1.92;1.93]

From the foregoing eight theorems the remaining principles of eductive equivalence follow so simply that they will be for the present omitted. They will all appear in the summary (Sec. 28).

25. Principles of Double Negation.

By a principle of double negation is meant a proposition of the form[1]

$$sXp \text{ is equivalent to } s''Xp$$

or of the form

$$sXp \text{ is equivalent to } sXp''.$$

2.21 sEp is equivalent to $s''Ep$
[1.2,$s/p,p/s$] pEs is equivalent to pEs'' (1)
[(1);2.12]   theorem

2.22 sAp is equivalent to sAp''
[1.2,p'/p] sEp' is equivalent to sEp''' (1)
[(1);1.91]   theorem

2.23 sAp is equivalent to $s''Ap$
[2.21,p'/p] sEp' is equivalent to $s''Ep'$ (1)
[(1);1.91]   theorem

2.24 sIp is equivalent to sIp''
[1.2] sEp is equivalent to sEp'' (1)
[(1)] sEp is false is equivalent to sEp'' is false (2)
[(2);1.92]   theorem

2.25 sIp is equivalent to $s''Ip$
                 Similarly [2.21;1.92]

2.26 sOp is equivalent to sOp''
                 Similarly [2.22;1.93]

---
[1] For the explanation of the symbols used in this definition see Sec. 21.

2.27 sOp is equivalent to $s''Op$
        Similarly [2.23;1.93]

In virtue of these seven theorems and of 1.2, any term may be replaced by its double negative and *vice versa*. The use of the principles of double negation will frequently be tacit.

26. The Principles of Contradiction. By a principle of contradiction is meant a proposition of the form[1]

$Y_1(s,p)$ is equivalent to $Y_2(s,p)$ *is false*.

2.31 sIp is equivalent to sEp *is false*
   [2.15] sIp is equivalent to sIp (1)
   [(1);1.92]   theorem

2.32 sEp is equivalent to sIp *is false*
        Similarly, or directly from 2.31

The remaining principles of contradiction follow so simply from these two that they are not given in the present section. They will all appear in the summary (Sec. 28).

27. Table of Propositional Forms. The following table is needed in our summary of the principles of equivalence (Sec. 28). The table consists of all the A, E, I, and O propositions the subject of which is s or s' and the predicate p or p', and all the A, E, I, and O propositions the subject of which is p or p' and the predicate s or s'. In other words it consists of all the values of the function $Y(s,p)$. They are arranged in eight groups of four. The significance of the grouping will appear shortly.

Table

Group I:	sEp	pEs	sAp'	pAs'
Group II:	$s'Ep$	pEs'	$s'Ap'$	pAs
Group III:	sEp'	$p'Es$	sAp	$p'As'$
Group IV:	$s'Ep'$	$p'Es'$	$s'Ap$	$p'As$
Group V:	sIp	pIs	sOp'	pOs'
Group VI:	$s'Ip$	pIs'	$s'Op'$	pOs
Group VII:	sIp'	$p'Is$	sOp	$p'Os'$
Group VIII:	$s'Ip'$	$p'Is'$	$s'Op$	$p'Os$

28. Summary of the Principles of Equivalence.

1. *Principles of eductive equivalence.* Every propositional form is equivalent to any propositional form in the same group (Sec. 27) as itself.

[1] For the explanation of the symbols used in this definition see Sec. 21.

2. *Principles of double negation.* Any form sXp is equivalent to sXp'' and to $s''Xp$. (Hence, any term may be replaced by its double negative and *vice versa.*)

3. *Principles of contradiction.*

(*a*) Any form in Group V is equivalent to the falsity of any form in Group I (and any form in Group I is equivalent to the falsity of any form in Group V). We may express this more briefly as follows : V is equivalent to not-I (and I is equivalent to not-V).

(*b*) VI is equivalent to not-II (and II is equivalent to not-VI).

(*c*) VII is equivalent to not-III (and III is equivalent to not-VII).

(*d*) VIII is equivalent to not-IV (and IV is equivalent to not-VIII).

That all of the statements comprised in the above summary follow from our postulates may be shown as follows.

1. *Principles of eductive equivalence.* That the forms in Group I are mutually equivalent follows from theorems 2.11–2.14. Writing s' for s in Group I, we get the forms of Group II, hence the forms of Group II are mutually equivalent. Similarly, writing p' for p in I, and s' for s and p' for p in I, we prove the same of III and of IV.

That the forms in Group V are mutually equivalent follows from theorems 2.15–2.18. Substituting in V as above we prove the same of VI, VII, and VIII.

2. *Principles of double negation.* This follows directly from postulate 1.2 and theorems 2.21–2.27.

3. *Principles of contradiction.*

(*a*) 2.31 states that sIp is equivalent to sEp *is false*. But sIp is a form in Group V and sEp a form in Group I. Hence in virtue of the mutual equivalence of forms in the same group, V is equivalent to not-I. (And this, by the meaning of equivalence, is equivalent to " I is equivalent to not-V.")

(*b*) Writing s' for s in V and I, we get VI and II respectively. Hence VI is equivalent to not-II.

(*c*) and (*d*) Similarly.

29. Definition of Eduction. By an eduction or eductive argument is meant a proposition of the form[1]
$$Y_1(s,p) \text{ implies } Y_2(s,p).$$

30. The Valid Moods[2] of Eduction.

2.41 sEp implies sEp

This follows from the meaning of implication.

2.42 sIp implies sIp

                Similarly

2.43 sEp implies $s'Ip$

[1.3] sEp implies $s'Ep$ is false   (1)

[(1);2.31,s'/s]   theorem

From these three moods all the other valid moods of eduction may be derived immediately by substitution (see Sec. 23). The following, which will be used in the sequel, will serve as an example.

2.44 sEp implies sIp'

[2.43,$s/p,p/s$] pEs implies $p'Is$ (1)

[(1);2.12;2.16]   theorem

All of the valid moods of eduction will appear in the summary (Sec. 32.)

31. The Invalid Moods of Eduction. Our theorems of invalidity are all stated elliptically. Take, for example, 2.51, which asserts that sEp does not imply sIp. Written in full, this theorem would be: It is false that for every element s and every element p sEp implies sIp. Similarly with all the other theorems of invalidity.

2.51 sEp does not imply sIp

[1.6]   There exist elements s and p such that

          sEp (1)

[2.32] sEp implies sIp is false   (2)

[(1);(2)] There exist elements s and p such that

          sEp and sIp is false   (3)

[(3)]   theorem

---

[1] For the explanation of the symbols used in this definition see Sec. 21.
[2] We follow Professor Singer in calling the forms of eduction "moods."

2.52 sEp does not imply $s'Ip'$

[1.6]	There exist elements s and p such that sEp	(1)
[1.5]	sEp implies pEp'	(2)
[2.32]	pEp' implies pIp' is false	(3)
[(1);(2);(3)]	There exists an element p such that pEp' and pIp' is false	(4)
[(4);2.12]	There exists an element p such that $p'Ep$ and pIp' is false	(5)
[(5)]	There exist elements s and p such that sEp and $s'Ip'$ is false[1]	(6)
[(6)]	theorem	

2.53 sEp does not imply $s'Ep'$

[1.4,$s'/s,m/p,p/m$]

	$s'Ep'$ and mEp implies $s'Em$	(1)

[(1);2.43,$s'/s,m/p$;2.25,m/p]

	$s'Ep'$ and mEp implies sIm	(2)
[(2)]	sIm is false and mEp implies $s'Ep'$ is false	(3)
[(3);2.32;2.31]	sEm and mEp implies $s'Ip'$	(4)
[1.6]	There exist elements s, m, and p such that sEm and mEp and sEp	(5)
[(4);(5)]	There exist elements s, m, and p such that sEm and mEp and sEp and $s'Ip'$	(6)
[(6)]	There exist elements s and p such that sEp and $s'Ip'$	(7)
[(7);2.31]	There exist elements s and p such that sEp and $s'Ep'$ is false	(8)
[(8)]	theorem	

2.54 sIp does not imply $s'Ip'$

Assume that sIp implies $s'Ip'$

Then [$s'/p,p'/s$;2.24;2.25]

	$s'Ip'$ implies sIp	
and	sIp is false implies $s'Ip'$ is false	
and [2.32]	sEp implies $s'Ep'$	
But [2.53]	sEp does not imply $s'Ep'$	
Hence	theorem	

[1] For example, let $s = p'$.

The next theorems follow *a fortiori* from those just proved.

2.55 sEp does not imply sEp'
    Assume that sEp implies sEp'
Then [2.44,p'/p;2.24]
    sEp implies sIp
But [2.51] sEp does not imply sIp
Hence   theorem

2.56 sIp does not imply sIp'
    Assume that sIp implies sIp'
Then [p'/p] sIp' implies sIp
and [2.44] sEp implies sIp
But [2.51] sEp does not imply sIp
Hence   theorem

2.57 sIp does not imply sEp
    Similarly [2.44;2.56]

2.58 sIp does not imply $s'Ep'$
    Similarly [2.43;2.56]

2.59 sIp does not imply sEp'
    Similarly [2.43;2.54]

The remaining theorems of eductive invalidity follow immediately by substitution from the foregoing nine theorems.

The process of term-substitution in theorems of invalidity calls for justification. For, let A_1 be any invalid form of argument and let A_2 be a form of argument which is derived from A_1 by term substitution : it is not immediately clear that A_2 must also be invalid. Indeed, if our term substitution is performed in such a way that two terms s and p in A_1 become identical in A_2 (for example, s and s respectively) or become one the negative of the other (for example, s' and s respectively) then it is possible that A_2 should be valid though A_1 is not.

However, in deriving theorems of invalidity simply by substitution from other theorems of invalidity, we never have any occasion to *identify* or *oppose* terms. By *identifying* terms, an expression which is due to Professor Singer, is meant substituting in such a way that two terms s and p in A_1 become identical in A_2 (become, for example, s and s respectively). By *opposing* terms is meant substituting in such a way that two terms s and p

in A_1 become in A_2 one the negative of the other (for example, s' and s).

Now, it can be shown easily that, when neither this identification nor opposition of terms is employed, if A_2 is derived by substitution from A_1, A_1 may also be derived by substitution from A_2, that hence A_1 and A_2 are equivalent, and that hence the invalidity of A_2 follows from the invalidity of A_1.

32. Summary of Eduction. The following summary of eduction is based upon the Table of Propositional Forms (Sec. 27).

1. *The Valid Moods*

(*a*) Any propositional form implies any form in the same group as itself.

(*b*) Any form in Group I implies any form in Group VI and implies any form in Group VII. We may express this more briefly as follows: I implies VI and VII.

(*c*) II implies V and VIII.

(*d*) III implies V and VIII.

(*e*) IV implies VI and VII.

2. *The Invalid Moods*

(*a*) I does not imply II, III, IV, V, or VIII.

(*b*) II does not imply I, III, IV, VI, or VII.

(*c*) III does not imply I, II, IV, VI, or VII.

(*d*) IV does not imply I, II, III, V, or VIII.

(*e*) V does not imply I, II, III, IV, VI, VII, or VIII.

(*f*) VI does not imply I, II, III, IV, V, VII, or VIII.

(*g*) VII does not imply I, II, III, IV, V, VI, or VIII.

(*h*) VIII does not imply I, II, III, IV, V, VI, or VII.

That every statement comprised in the above summary follows from the postulates may be seen as follows.

1. *The Valid Moods*

(*a*) We have already shown that any form is equivalent to any form in the same group. *A fortiori* any form implies any form in the same group.

(*b*) sEp implies sIp' (2.44). But sEp belongs to Group I and sIp' to Group VII. Therefore, in view of the mutual equivalence of forms in the same group, I implies VII. Similarly, since sEp implies $s'Ip$ (2.43), I implies VI.

(c) Similarly, writing s' for s in 2.43 and in 2.44 we show that II implies V and VIII.

(d) This step is proved by writing p' for p in 2.44 and 2.43.

(e) And this by writing s' for s and p' for p.

2. *The Invalid Moods*

The proof of this part of the summary is analogous to the foregoing and is omitted.

Accordingly, since the summary is obviously complete, every arithmetically possible mood of eduction is such that either it or its invalidity is deducible from the postulates.

33. Alternative Summary of Eduction. I now wish to give an alternative summary, one which has already been hinted at and which will be very useful later.

For this purpose we must define " of the same type."[1] Two forms of argument are said to be of the same type when the premise (or premises) of the one is equivalent to the premise (or premises) of the other and the conclusion of the one is equivalent to the conclusion of the other, or when by means of term substitution throughout the one (provided that terms be neither identified nor opposed) a form of argument can be constructed whose premise (or premises) is equivalent to the premise (or premises) of the other and whose conclusion is equivalent to the conclusion of the other.

We may now summarize eduction as follows:

The valid moods of eduction are 2.41, 2.42, and 2.44[2] and other moods of the same type as any one of these.

The invalid moods of eduction are those declared invalid by theorems 2.51–2.59 and other moods of the same type as any one of these.

That all of the statements comprised in the above summary follow from the postulates is obvious. What remains to be proved is the completeness of this summary. Is every arithmetically possible mood of eduction covered by this summary?

Let us begin by noticing the character of the three moods which are established by 2.41, 2.42, and 2.44 and the nine which

---

[1] The phrase " of the same type," as used in this book, does *not* refer to the " theory of types."

[2] It will be convenient to use 2.44 rather than 2.43 in this summary.

are declared invalid by 2.51–2.59. These twelve moods are the arithmetically possible ones which can be constructed by taking either *sEp* or *sIp* as premise, and either *sEp*, *sIp*, *sEp'*, *sIp'*, *s'Ep'*, or *s'Ip'* as conclusion.

Now if we write *s* for *p* and *p* for *s* and then simply convert the premise and conclusion in 2.44, 2.55, 2.56, and 2.59 we arrive at the four moods in which either *sEp* or *sIp* is premise and either *s'Ep* or *s'Ip* is conclusion. These four moods together with the original twelve make the sixteen arithmetically possible ones which can be arrived at by taking either *sEp* or *sIp* as premise and restricting the moods to what we may call the " first figure "[1] (*i.e.* the arrangement of terms in which *s* or *s'* is subject and *p* or *p'* is predicate of both premise and conclusion).—Now if we write *s* for *s'* throughout each of these sixteen moods, we arrive obviously at the sixteen arithmetically possible ones which can be arrived at by taking either *s'Ep* or *s'Ip* as premise and restricting the moods to the first figure.—Then by writing *p'* for *p*, and finally *s'* for *s* and *p'* for *p* in our first sixteen moods, we get thirty-two more. The sixty-four moods, which we now have, obviously exhaust the possibilities of the first figure where the premise is either *E* or *I* and the conclusion is either *E* or *I*.

From these sixty-four moods all of the moods not in the first figure but whose premise is either *E* or *I* and whose conclusion is either *E* or *I* can be derived, in virtue of the fact that *E* and *I* are simply convertible (*i.e.* are equivalent to their simple converses).

Finally, *every* mood of eduction is equivalent to one whose premise is either *E* or *I* and whose conclusion is either *E* or *I*, because every *A* proposition is equivalent to an *E* proposition and every *O* proposition is equivalent to an *I* proposition (by obversion).

Hence our original twelve moods and those which are of the same type as any of these constitute an exhaustive list of the moods of eduction.

From this it follows that every arithmetically possible mood of eduction is such that either it or its invalidity is deducible from the postulates.

[1] The application of the notion of " figure " to eduction is due to Professor Singer.

34. Definition of Opposition. Opposition is ordinarily defined in an inconveniently narrow fashion.

By an oppositional argument we shall mean an argument of the form[1]

$$Z_1(s,p) \text{ implies } Z_2(s,p).$$

The problem of opposition is accordingly the following. Suppose we choose any two propositional forms, f and g, from the table in Sec. 27. Now there are four questions which we might ask about them: (1) does f imply g? (2) does f imply g *is false*? (3) does f *is false* imply g? (4) does f *is false* imply g *is false*? To answer each of these questions for every form f in the table and every form g in the table is the business of the doctrine of opposition.

35. Theorems of Opposition. Now all of the theorems of opposition are included either in our treatment of eduction or in our treatment of the principles of contradiction, or are immediately derivable from the theorems of eduction by an application of one or two of the principles of contradiction.

Hence we need only give a summary of opposition.

36. Summary of Opposition. The most convenient method of summarizing opposition is by means of the relations of contradiction, contrariety, subcontrariety, and subalternation, which are the four relations ordinarily used in discussing opposition, and three further relations which we shall call superalternation, correspondence, and supplementation.

We begin by defining these notions. The definitions will be formulated in such a way that the completeness of our summary will be immediately clear; the fulfilment of this purpose requires a certain amount of redundancy in the definitions; footnotes will point out what clauses are redundant. Let f and g be any propositional forms chosen from the table in Sec. 27; then:

f is said to be *contradictory* to g when (1) f does not imply g, (2) f implies g *is false*, (3) f *is false* implies g, and (4) f *is false* does not imply g *is false*.[2]

---

[1] For the meaning of the symbols used in this definition see Sec. 21.
[2] Clauses (1) and (4) are redundant.

f is said to be *contrary* to *g* when (1) *f* does not imply *g*, (2) *f* implies *g is false*, (3) *f is false* does not imply *g*, (4) *f is false* does not imply *g is false*.[1]

f is said to be *subcontrary* to *g* when (1) *f* does not imply *g*, (2) *f* does not imply *g is false*, (3) *f is false* implies *g*, (4) *f is false* does not imply *g is false*.[2]

It follows from the definitions just given that contradiction, contrariety, and subcontrariety are each symmetrical; for example, if *f* is contradictory to *g*, *g* is contradictory to *f*.

f is said to be *subalternate* to *g* when (1) *f* does not imply *g*, (2) *f* does not imply *g is false*, (3) *f is false* does not imply *g*, and (4) *f is false* implies *g is false*.[3]

f is said to be *superalternate* to *g* when (1) *f* implies *g*, (2) *f* does not imply *g is false*, (3) *f is false* does not imply *g*, and (4) *f is false* does not imply *g is false*.[4]

The relations of subalternation and superalternation are asymmetrical; that is, if *f* is subalternate to *g*, *g* is not subalternate to *f*.

f is said to be *correspondent* to *g* when (1) *f* implies *g*, (2) *f* does not imply *g is false*, (3) *f is false* does not imply *g*, and (4) *f is false* implies *g is false*.[5] (This relation is the same as equivalence.)

f is said to be *supplementary* to *g* when (1) *f* does not imply *g*, (2) *f* does not imply *g is false*, (3) *f is false* does not imply *g*, and (4) *f is false* does not imply *g is false*.

The relations of correspondence and supplementation are symmetrical.

We may now give our summary of opposition. The simplest way is to give it in the form of a table. The table reads in the usual direction. Roman numerals stand for the " groups " in Sec. 27. The Arabic numerals are explained immediately after the table.

---

[1] (1) and (4) are redundant.
[2] (1) and (4) are redundant.
[3] (2) and (3) are redundant.
[4] (2) and (3) are redundant.
[5] (2) and (3) are redundant.

Table of Opposition

	I	II	III	IV	V	VI	VII	VIII
I	1	3	3	7	2	6	6	7
II	3	1	7	3	6	2	7	6
III	3	7	1	3	6	7	2	6
IV	7	3	3	1	7	6	6	2
V	2	5	5	7	1	4	4	7
VI	5	2	7	5	4	1	7	4
VII	5	7	2	5	4	7	1	4
VIII	7	5	5	2	7	4	4	1

1 = "is correspondent to"
2 = "is contradictory to"
3 = "is contrary to"
4 = "is subcontrary to"
5 = "is subalternate to"
6 = "is superalternate to"
7 = "is supplementary to"

CHAPTER III

MEDIATE INFERENCE

37. Definition of Syllogism. By a syllogism is meant an argument of the form[1]

$Y_1(s,m)$ and $Y_2(m,p)$ implies $Y_3(s,p)$.

This definition, one should note, is wider than that ordinarily given; it covers arguments which involve negative terms, for example the argument *sEm'* and *mAp* implies *sAp*, as well as arguments of the kind which are ordinarily called syllogisms and which do not contain negative terms.

38. The Valid Moods of the Syllogism.

3.11	*sEm'* and *mEp* implies *sEp*		
	[1.4]	*sEm'* and *pEm* implies *sEp*	(1)
	[(1);2.12]	theorem	
3.12	*sEm'* and *mEp* implies *sIp'*		
	[3.11]	*sEm'* and *mEp* implies *sEp*	(1)
	[2.44]	*sEp* implies *sIp'*	(2)
	[(1);(2)]	theorem	
3.13	*sIm* and *mEp* implies *sIp'*		
	[1.4,*p*/*m*,*m*/*p*]	*sEp'* and *mEp* implies *sEm*	(1)
	[(1)]	*sEm* is false and *mEp* implies *sEp'* is false	(2)
	[(2);1.92]	theorem	
3.14	*sEm* and *mEp* implies *s'Ip'*		
	[3.13,*s'*/*s*]	*s'Im* and *mEp* implies *s'Ip'*	(1)
	[2.43]	*sEm* implies *s'Im*	(2)
	[(1);(2)]	theorem	

From these four theorems all of the other forms of valid syllogism, including of course the twenty-four standard forms, may be derived immediately by substitution.

39. Consequences of Postulate 1.5. Before deducing our syllogistic theorems of invalidity, we must derive certain consequences of postulates 1.5, which will be used frequently from now on.

[1] For the explanation of the symbols used in this definition see Sec. 21.

3.21 sEp implies $p'Ep$
        [1.5] sEp implies pEp' (1)
        [(1);2.12]   theorem
3.22 sEp implies sEs'
        [1.5,$s/p,p/s$] pEs implies sEs' (1)
        [(1);2.12]   theorem
3.23 sEp implies $s'Es$
                           [3.22;2.12]

40. Invalid Moods of the Syllogism.

3.31 sEm and mEp does not imply sIp
        [1.6]   There exist elements s, m, and p such
                           that sEm and mEp and sEp (1)
        [2.32] sEp is equivalent to sIp is false   (2)
        [(1);(2)]   There exist elements s, m, and p such
                           that sEm and mEp and sIp is false (3)
        [(3)]   theorem
3.32 sEm' and mEp does not imply $s'Ep'$
        [2.41] sEp implies sEp (1)
        [3.21] sEp implies $p'Ep$ (2)
        [(1);(2)] sEp implies sEp and $p'Ep$ (3)
        Now assume that
                           sEm' and mEp implies $s'Ep'$
        Then [p'/m] sEp and $p'Ep$ implies $s'Ep'$ (4)
        and [(3);(4)] sEp implies $s'Ep'$ (5)
        But [2.53] sEp does not imply $s'Ep'$ (6)
        Hence [(5);(6)]   theorem
3.33 sEm' and mEp does not imply sIp
                           Similarly [3.21;2.51]
3.34 sEm' and mEp does not imply $s'Ip'$
                           Similarly [3.21;2.52]
3.35 sEm and mEp does not imply sIp'
        Assume that sEm and mEp implies sIp' (1)
        Then [$m/p,p/m$] sEp and pEm implies sIm' (2)
        and [2.12] sEp and mEp implies sIm' (3)
        and [(3)] sIm' is false and mEp implies sEp is
                           false   (4)

	and [(4);2.32;2.31]	(5)
	sEm' and *mEp* implies *sIp*	
But [3.33]	*sEm'* and *mEp* does not imply *sIp*	(6)
Hence [(5);(6)]	theorem	

3.36 *sIm'* and *mEp* does not imply *s'Ip'*

Assume that   *sIm'* and *mEp* implies *s'Ip'*
Then [*m*/*p*,*p*/*m*,*s'*/*s*]

	s'Ip' and *pEm* implies *sIm'*	(1)
and [(1);2.12]	*s'Ip'* and *mEp* implies *sIm'*	(2)
and [(2)]	*sIm'* is false and *mEp* implies *s'Ip'* is false	(3)
and [(3);2.32]	*sEm'* and *mEp* implies *s'Ep'*	(4)
But [3.32]	*sEm'* and *mEp* does not imply *s'Ep'*	(5)
Hence	theorem	

The next theorems (3.41–3.466) follow *a fortiori* from those which have just been proved (3.31–3.36). That is to say, the next theorems are derived by strengthening the conclusion or weakening a premise of the foregoing theorems.

3.41 *sEm'* and *mEp* does not imply *sEp'*

[3.34]	*sEm'* and *mEp* does not imply *s'Ip'*	(1)
[2.43]	*sEp'* implies *s'Ip'*	(2)
[(1);(2)]	theorem	

3.421 *sEm* and *mEp* does not imply *sEp*
                 Similarly [3.35;2.44]

3.422 *sEm* and *mEp* does not imply *sEp'*
                 Similarly [3.31;2.44,*p'*/*p*]

3.423 *sEm* and *mEp* does not imply *s'Ep'*
                 Similarly [3.35;2.43,*s'*/*s*]

3.431 *sIm* and *mEp* does not imply *sIp*

[3.33]	*sEm'* and *mEp* does not imply *sIp*	(1)
[2.44,*m'*/*p*]	*sEm'* implies *sIm*	(2)
[(1);(2)]	theorem	

3.432 *sIm* and *mEp* does not imply *s'Ip'*
                 Similarly [3.34;2.44,*m'*/*p*]

3.433 *sIm* and *mEp* does not imply *s'Ip*
                 Similarly [3.31,*s'*/*s*;2.43,*s'*/*s*,*m*/*p*]

3.434 *sIm* and *mEp* does not imply *sEp'*
                 Similar to proof of 3.41 [3.431]

3.435 sIm and mEp does not imply $s'Ep$
Similarly [3.431]

3.436 sIm and mEp does not imply sEp
Similarly [3.433]

3.437 sIm and mEp does not imply $s'Ep'$
Similarly [3.433]

3.441 sIm' and mEp does not imply sIp
Similar to proof of 3.431 [3.31]

3.442 sIm' and mEp does not imply sIp'
Similarly [3.35]

3.443 sIm' and mEp does not imply $s'Ip$
Similarly [3.33,s'/s]

3.444 sIm' and mEp does not imply sEp
Similar to proof of 3.41 [3.443]

3.445 sIm' and mEp does not imply $s'Ep'$
Similarly [3.442]

3.446 sIm' and mEp does not imply sEp'
Similarly [3.441]

3.447 sIm' and mEp does not imply $s'Ep$
Similarly [3.441]

3.451 sIm and mIp does not imply $s'Ip'$
Similar to proof of 3.431 [3.36,m'/m]

3.452 sIm and mIp does not imply sIp'
Similarly [3.442,m'/m]

3.453 sIm and mIp does not imply sIp
Similarly [3.441,m'/m]

3.454 sIm and mIp does not imply sEp'
Similar to proof of 3.41 [3.453]

3.455 sIm and mIp does not imply $s'Ep'$
Similarly [3.452]

3.456 sIm and mIp does not imply sEp
Similarly [3.452]

3.461 sIm' and mIp does not imply sIp
Similar to proof of 3.431 [3.442,p'/p]

3.462 sIm' and mIp does not imply sIp'
Similarly [3.441,p'/p]

3.463 sIm' and mIp does not imply $s'Ip'$
Similarly [3.443,p'/p]

3.464 sIm' and mIp does not imply sEp
        Similar to proof of 3.41 [3.462]
3.465 sIm' and mIp does not imply sEp'
        Similarly [3.463]
3.466 sIm' and mIp does not imply $s'Ep'$
        Similarly [3.462]

From the foregoing all the remaining principles of invalidity may be derived immediately by substitution. The following is given a number since it is used frequently in the sequel.

3.471 sEm and mEp does not imply $s'Ip$

41. Summary of Syllogism. The method which was used in our first summary of eduction can be applied to the syllogism. But in the case of the syllogism it is exceedingly cumbersome. The method of our alternative summary of eduction is here by far the more convenient.

Summary of valid moods. The following are the valid moods of the syllogism: 3.11–3.14 and all other moods of the same type[1] as any one of these.

Summary of invalid moods. The following are the invalid moods of the syllogism: the moods declared invalid by 3.31–3.466 and all other moods of the same type as any one of these.

The proof of the summary—and of the completeness of our treatment of the syllogism—is so similar to that of our proof of the alternative summary of eduction that it is omitted.

42. Introduction to the Sorites. We now turn to the sorites. We shall first define this species of argument. Then, to illustrate the methods used in dealing with the sorites, we shall give a complete treatment of the sorites with *three* premises. Finally, we shall show that these methods may be extended to the sorites with n premises and that the validity or invalidity of every sorites, no matter how many premises it may have, is determined by the postulates.

43. Definition of the Sorites. In treating the sorites, we shall find it convenient to use the letter a with subscripts, instead of s, m, and p, to stand for terms.

---
[1] For the meaning of the phrase "of the same type" see Sec. 33.

A sorites is an argument of the form[1]
$Y_1(a_0,a_1)$ and $Y_2(a_1,a_2)$ and ... and $Y_n(a_{n-1},a_n)$
implies $Y_{n-1}(a_0,a_n)$ $(n>1)$.
According to this definition, a syllogism is a special case of the sorites: it is a sorites with two premises. Whether the syllogism be thus treated as one kind of sorites, or as a form coördinate with the sorites, is a matter of little importance. Readers who prefer that the syllogism should not be considered as a species of sorites need only specify in the above definition that n shall be greater than 2.

44. The Sorites with Three Premises: Valid Moods.

3.51 a_0Ea_1' and a_1Ea_2' and a_2Ea_3 implies a_0Ea_3
[3.11] a_0Ea_1' and a_1Ea_2' implies a_0Ea_2' (1)
[3.11] a_0Ea_2' and a_2Ea_3 implies a_0Ea_3 (2)
[(1);(2)]   theorem

3.52 a_0Ea_1' and a_1Ea_2' and a_2Ea_3 implies a_0Ia_3'
[3.51;2.44]

3.53 a_0Ea_1 and a_1Ea_2' and a_2Ea_3 implies $a_0'Ia_3'$
[3.14;3.13]

3.54 a_0Ia_1 and a_1Ea_2' and a_2Ea_3 implies a_0Ia_3'
[3.13]

3.55 a_0Ea_1 and a_1Ia_2 and a_2Ea_3 implies $a_0'Ia_3'$
[3.13]

From these valid moods (3.51–3.55) all the other valid moods of the sorites with three premises may be derived immediately by substitution.

45. The Sorites with Three Premises: Invalid Moods.

We now come to that part of our system which is at once the most difficult and theoretically the most interesting. The problem which now confronts us is this: how can the invalidity of any invalid sorites be deduced from the postulates? At first glance this might seem to be an insoluble problem. For, while it is easy to see how we may work *upwards* from principles of validity to other principles of validity of *greater* complexity and *downwards* from principles of invalidity to other principles of invalidity of *less* complexity, it is not easy to see how we may work

---

[1] For the explanation of the symbols used in this definition see Sec. 21.

upwards from principles of invalidity or *downwards* from principles of validity. The problem, however, is soluble. Its solution, which is a notable contribution to Aristotelian logic, was first given by Professor Singer.[1]

We shall not, however, be able to use his method in precisely the form in which he propounded it, because our postulate 1.5 is weaker than the corresponding postulate in his system. Our method, which is a modification of his, is already familiar to the reader from the proofs of various theorems in Sec. 40; it consists in the employment of 1.5, 3.21, 3.22, or 3.23 in a *reductio ad absurdum* argument.

3.61 a_0Ea_1' and a_1Ea_2' and a_2Ea_3 does not imply a_0Ia_3

[3.21;2.21] a_0Ea_1' implies a_1Ea_1' (1)

[(1);2.41] a_0Ea_1' and a_1Ea_3 implies a_0Ea_1' and a_1Ea_1' and a_1Ea_3 (2)

Assume that a_0Ea_1' and a_1Ea_2' and a_2Ea_3 implies a_0Ia_3

Then $[a_1/a_2]$ a_0Ea_1' and a_1Ea_1' and a_1Ea_3 implies a_0Ia_3 (3)

and [(2);(3)] a_0Ea_1' and a_1Ea_3 implies a_0Ia_3 (4)

But [3.33] a_0Ea_1' and a_1Ea_3 does not imply a_0Ia_3 (5)

Hence [(4);(5)] theorem

3.62 a_0Ea_1' and a_1Ea_2' and a_2Ea_3 does not imply $a_0'Ia_3'$
     Similarly [3.34]

3.63 a_0Ea_1' and a_1Ea_2' and a_2Ea_3 does not imply $a_0'Ea_3'$
     Similarly [3.32]

3.64 a_0Ea_1' and a_1Ea_2 and a_2Ea_3 does not imply a_0Ia_3
     Similarly [3.31]

3.65 a_0Ea_1' and a_1Ea_2 and a_2Ea_3 does not imply a_0Ia_3'
     Similarly [3.35]

3.66 a_0Ea_1' and a_1Ea_2 and a_2Ea_3 does not imply $a_0'Ia_3$
     Similarly [3.471]

3.67 a_0Ea_1 and a_1Ea_2 and a_2Ea_3 does not imply a_0Ia_3
     Similarly [3.33]

3.68 a_0Ea_1 and a_1Ea_2 and a_2Ea_3 does not imply $a_0'Ia_3'$
     Similarly [3.34]

---

[1] Cf. H. B. Smith: *Letters on Logic*, pp. 51-2.

3.69 a_0Ea_1 and a_1Ea_2 and a_2Ea_3 does not imply a_0Ia_3'
Similarly [3.31]

In a completely detailed account of the sorites with three premises, we should now proceed to deduce theorems which follow *a fortiori* from those which have just been proved. As this procedure would be exactly parallel to the deduction of the syllogistic theorems 3.41–3.466, it is here omitted. We should thus arrive at a set of theorems from which all the remaining invalid forms of the sorites with three premises could be derived immediately by substitution.

Hence the validity or invalidity of every sorites with three premises is determined by the postulates.

46. Introduction to the Sorites with n Premises. Obviously, the methods which have been used in treating the sorites with three premises can be extended to the sorites with any number of premises. By successive steps, valid forms of the sorites of any desired degree of complexity may be built up. Also, by succsssive applications of 1.5 or its consequences, an invalid sorites of any length may be broken down to any desired extent.

It is not obvious, however, that *every* sorites must yield to these methods. There might be a sorites which on the one hand could not be constructed from valid syllogisms, and which on the other hand though it could be broken down *ad libitum* yet could not be broken down into a demonstrably invalid argument. Such a sorites would not be determined for validity or invalidity by the postulates ; or at least the methods which we have been using would not be adequate.

That there is no such sorites we must now prove. We must show that the validity or invalidity of every sorites is determined by the postulates and can be demonstrated by methods which we have already used.

We shall do this by means of a summary. We shall give a summary of the valid and invalid kinds of the sorites with n premises, a summary which will obviously exhaust all the possibilities, and each step of which will be proved.

47. Definitions.[1] We must first define certain expressions which will be used in our summary.

1. The *major term* of a sorites is the predicate of the conclusion. The *major premise* of a sorites is the premise a term of which is identical with or is opposed to (*i.e.* is the negative of) the major term.

2. The *minor term* of a sorites is the subject of the conclusion. The *minor premise* of a sorites is the premise a term of which is identical with or is opposed to the minor term.

3. A *middle term* of a sorites is a term of one of the premises and is neither identical with nor opposed to the major term or the minor term. A *middle premise* is a premise which is neither the major nor the minor premise.

4. By a *pair of terms* is meant two opposed terms (a and a') or two identical terms (a and a).

5. Two opposed terms a and a' are said to *disagree*. Two identical terms a and a are said to *agree*. When the terms composing a pair of terms disagree, we shall say that the *pair disagrees*. When the terms composing a pair of terms agree, we shall say that the *pair agrees*.

Thus, in the sorites $a_0 E a_1$ and $a_1' E a_2$ and $a_2 E a_3$ implies $a_0' E a_3'$, the first premise is the minor premise, the second is the middle premise, and the third is the major premise. The predicate of the minor premise (a_1) and the subject of the middle premise (a_1') together constitute a pair of middle terms; this pair disagrees. The predicate of the middle premise (a_2) and the subject of the major premise (a_2) together constitute a pair of middle terms; this pair agrees. The terms of the conclusion (a_0' and a_3') both disagree with terms of the premises (namely, a_0 and a_3).

---

[1] In the present section we are somewhat bothered by an ambiguity in the word "term." This ambiguity may be best pointed out by an illustration. Take the syllogism in *Barbara*: sAm and mAp implies sAp. How many *terms* does it contain? In one sense of the word "term" *Barbara* contains six terms, namely, the subject and predicate of the major premise the subject and predicate of the minor premise, and the subject and predicate of the conclusion. In another sense, however, it contains but three terms, namely, s, m, and p. This ambiguity need cause little trouble once these two meanings have been distinguished, for the intended meaning is usually clear in a given context. To avoid any possible misunderstanding, however, I state that throughout the definitions given in the present section the first of these two meanings is intended.

6. By *elimination* we shall mean the process of dropping a premise by means of the identification or opposition of terms and in virtue of 1.5 or one of its consequences—the method used in Sec. 45.

48. Summary of the Valid Kinds of Sorites. The following are the valid kinds of sorites :

1. All moods of the sorites in which the premises are all E forms, the conclusion is an E form, each pair of middle terms disagrees, and each term of the conclusion agrees with a term of a premise ; and all moods the premises and conclusion of which are equivalent respectively to the premises and conclusion of any one of these moods.

Proof. Let us begin by proving the following theorem :
$a_0 E a_1'$ and $a_1 E a_2'$ ... and $a_{n-1} E a_n'$ implies $a_0 E a_n'$
for all values of n ($n > 1$)

This may be shown by mathematical induction as follows :

[3.11] $a_0 E a_1'$ and $a_1 E a_2'$ implies $a_0 E a_2'$ (1)

[2.41]   If $a_0 E a_1'$ and $a_1 E a_2'$ ... and $a_{n-1} E a'_n$ implies $a_0 E a_n'$ then $a_0 E a_1$ and $a_1 E a_2'$ ... and $a_{n-1} E a'_n$ and $a_n E a'_{n+1}$ implies $a_0 E a'_n$ and $a_n E a_n'{}_{+1}$ (2)

[3.11] $a_0 E a_n'$ and $a_n E a_n'{}_{+1}$ implies $a_0 E a_n'{}_{+1}$ (3)

[(2);(3)]   If $a_0 E a_1'$ and $a_1 E a_2'$ ... and $a_{n-1} E a_n'$ implies $a_0 E a_n'$ then $a_0 E a_1'$ and $a_1 E a_2'$ ... and $a_n E a_n'{}_{+1}$ implies $a_0 E a_n'{}_{+1}$ (4)

[(1);(4)]   theorem

From this it follows (in virtue of 1.1, the principle of double negation, and the convertibility of the E form) that all moods of the sorites in which the premises are E forms, the conclusion is an E form, each pair of middle terms disagrees, and each term of the conclusion agrees with a term of a premise, are valid. That all moods the premises and conclusion of which are equivalent respectively to the premises and conclusion of any one of these moods are valid follows from the meaning of equivalence.

2. All moods of the sorites in which the premises are all E forms, the conclusion an I form, each pair of middle terms disagrees, and one term of the conclusion agrees and one term of the conclusion disagrees with a term of a premise ; and all moods

the premises and conclusion of which are equivalent respectively to the premises and conclusion of any one of these moods.

Proof. This follows from 1 in virtue of 2.43 and 2.44.

3. All moods of the sorites in which the premises are all E forms, the conclusion an I form, one pair of middle terms agrees and the other pairs of middle terms disagree, and both terms of the conclusion disagree with terms of the premises; and all moods the premises and conclusion of which are equivalent respectively to the premises and conclusion of any one of these moods.

Proof. In any sorites of this kind, interchange the conclusion and one of the premises whose middle term agrees with the middle term of another premise, and contradict (*i.e.* write E for I, and I for E) the two forms which have been interchanged. The resulting sorites is then equivalent to the original sorites. But it is also equivalent to a sorites of the kind described in 2 above. Hence the original sorites is valid.

4. All moods of the sorites in which either the major or minor premise (but not both) is an I form, the other premises are E forms, the conclusion is I, the middle term contained in the I premise agrees with a term in another premise, all the other pairs of middle terms disagree, one term of the conclusion agrees with a term in the particular premise, and the other term of the conclusion disagrees with a term of a premise; and all moods the premises and conclusion of which are equivalent respectively to the premises and conclusion of any one of these moods.

Proof. Interchange the particular premise and the conclusion, and contradict these interchanged forms. The resulting sorites will be equivalent to the original one, and also to a sorites of the kind described in 1 above.

5. All moods of the sorites in which a middle premise is I, the other premises are E, the conclusion is I, each middle term of the I premise agrees with a term in another premise, the other pairs of middle terms disagree, and the terms of the conclusion both disagree with terms of the premises; and all moods the premises and conclusion of which are equivalent respectively to the premises and conclusion of any one of these moods.

Proof. Same as the proof of 4.

49. Lemmas. To prove various steps in our summary of the invalid kinds of sorites the following lemmas are required. As the proofs of these lemmas are long but not difficult they are omitted.

Lemma 1. Let S be any sorites with all of the following properties: (a) all of the premises of S are E forms; (b) the conclusion of S is either an E or an I form; and (c) at least one pair of middle terms of S disagrees.—Let l be the number of pairs of middle terms of S which agree; let m be the number of pairs of middle terms of S which disagree; and let n be the number of premises of S.—Now let a premise (of S) having a term which disagrees with a term of another premise (of S) be eliminated[1]; and let the resulting argument be called T.—Then T will have the following properties: (a) the number of pairs of middle terms of T which agree will be l; (b) the number of pairs of middle terms of T which disagree will be m-1; (c) the number of E premises of T will be n-1; (d) the terms of the conclusion of T will be related to terms of the premises of T in the same way[2] that the terms of the conclusion of S are related to terms of the premises of S; and (e) if the conclusion of S is an E form, the conclusion of T will be an E form, and, if the conclusion of S is an I form, the conclusion of T will be an I form.

Lemma 2. Let S be any sorites with all of the following properties: (a) all of the premises of S are E forms; (b) the conclusion of S is either an E or an I form; and (c) all of the pairs of middle terms of S agree.—Let n be the number of premises of S.—Now let the minor premise of S be eliminated; and let the resulting argument be called T.—Then T will have the following properties: (a) the number of pairs of middle terms of T which agree will be n-2; (b) the number of E premises of T will be n-1; (c) if the conclusion of S is an E form, the conclusion of T will be an E form, and, if the conclusion of S is an I form, the conclusion of T will be an I form; (d) the minor term (in the conclusion) of T will be related to a term in the minor premise of T in the opposite way[3] from that in which the minor

---
[1] In the sense defined in Sec. 47, 6.
[2] In respect to agreement and disagreement.
[3] In respect to agreement and disagreement.

term (in the conclusion) of S is related to a term in the minor premise of S; and (e) the major term (in the conclusion) of T will be related to a term in the major premise of T in the same way that the major term (in the conclusion) of S is related to a term in the major premise of S.

Lemma 3. Lemma 3 is the same as lemma 2 with " major " written for " minor " and " minor " for " major " throughout.

50. Summary of the Invalid Kinds of Sorites. The following are the invalid kinds of sorites:

1. All moods of the sorites in which the premises are of the kind described in 1, Sec. 48, and in which the conclusion is an I form both of whose terms agree with terms in the premises (Case I) or an I form both of whose terms disagree with terms of the premises (Case II) or an E form both of whose terms disagree with terms of the premises (Case III) or an E form one of whose terms agrees and the other disagrees with terms in the premises (Case IV); and all moods the premises and conclusion of which are equivalent respectively to the premises and conclusion of any one of these moods.

Proof.

Case I. By successive applications of 1.5 any sorites of this kind may be reduced to a syllogism, in which the premises are E forms, the middle terms disagree, the conclusion is an I form, and the terms of the conclusion agree with the terms of the premises (lemma 1). But all syllogisms of this type are invalid (3.33). Hence every sorites of this kind is invalid.

Case II. Similarly (3.34).
Case III. Similarly (3.32).
Case IV. Similarly (3.41); or *a fortiori* from Case I.

2. All moods of the sorites whose premises are of the kind described in 3, Sec. 48, and whose conclusion is an I form, the terms of which agree with terms of the premises (Case I) or an I form one of whose terms agrees and one disagrees with terms of the premises (Case II) or an E form (Case III); and all moods the premises and conclusions of which are equivalent respectively to the premises and conclusion of any one of these moods.

Proof.

Case I. Every sorites of this kind may be reduced to a syllogism in which the premises are both E, the middle terms agree, and the conclusion is an I whose terms agree with terms of the premises (lemma 1). But every syllogism of this type is invalid (3.31).

Case II.   Similarly (3.35).
Case III.   Similarly (3.421;3.422;3.423); or *a fortiori* from Cases I and II.

3. All moods of the sorites whose premises are all E forms, and whose pairs of middle terms all agree ; and all moods the premises and conclusion of which are equivalent respectively to the premises and conclusion of any one of these moods.

Proof.

Case I. Where the conclusion is an I form both of whose terms agree with terms in the premises.

If there are an even number of premises, then by successive applications of 1.5 the sorites can be reduced to a syllogism in which the premises are both E forms, the middle terms both agree, and the conclusion is an I form both of whose terms agree with terms in the premises (lemma 2). But all syllogisms of this type are invalid (3.31).

If there are an odd number of premises, then by successive applications of 1.5 the sorites can be reduced to a syllogism in which the premises are both E forms, the middle terms both agree, and the conclusion is an I form one of whose terms agrees and one of whose terms disagrees with terms of the premises (lemma 2). But all syllogisms of this type are invalid (3.35 and 3.471).

Case II. Where the conclusion is an I form both of whose terms disagree with terms in the premises.

If there are an even number of premises, the sorites can be reduced to a syllogism in which the premises are both E's, the middle terms both agree, and the conclusion is an I the terms of which both agree with terms in the premises (lemmas 2 and 3). But all syllogisms of this type are invalid (3.31).

If there are an odd number of premises, the sorites can be

reduced to a syllogism in which the premises are both E's, the middle terms both agree, and the conclusion is an I one of whose terms agrees and one of whose terms disagrees with terms of the premises (lemma 2). But all syllogisms of this type are invalid (3.35;3.471).

Case III. Where the conclusion is an I form one of whose terms disagrees with a term in the premises and one agrees.

Proof analogous to Cases I and II.

Cases IV–VI. Where the conclusion is an E form.

Proof a fortiori from Cases I–III.

4. All moods of the sorites whose premises are all E forms, and in which two or more pairs of middle terms agree, and one or more disagrees; and all moods the premises and conclusion of which are equivalent respectively to the premises and conclusion of any one of these moods.

Proof. Every sorites of this kind may be reduced to a sorites of the kind described in 3 (lemma 1).

5. All moods of the sorites at least one of whose premises is an I, and which differ in some respect from those described in 4 and 5, Sec. 48; and all moods the premises and conclusion of which are equivalent respectively to the premises and conclusion of any one of these moods.

Proof a fortiori from 1, 2, 3, and 4 this section.

51. The Sorites: Conclusion. An inspection of Secs. 48 and 50 will show that every possible kind of sorites has been covered. Hence every sorites is either deducibly valid or deducibly invalid from our postulates.

CHAPTER IV

COMPLETION OF THE SYSTEM

52. Introduction. In the foregoing chapters we claimed to have given a *complete* systematization of the various parts of Aristotelian logic. By means of our proved summaries we claimed to have shown that the validity or invalidity of *every* mood of eduction, syllogism, and sorites follows from the postulates. These claims, however, were somewhat exaggerated, as we now wish to point out.

What we did succeed in showing was this: that the validity or invalidity of every *normal* mood of eduction, syllogism, and sorites is deducible from the postulates. What we did not show is the deducibility of the validity or invalidity of every *telescoped* mood of eduction, syllogism, and sorites.

The purpose of the present chapter is to explain the distinction between *normal* and *telescoped* moods, and to indicate a complete treatment of the telescoped moods of the various species of argument. We shall see that our postulates, as they stand, are not competent to yield a complete treatment of telescoped arguments; accordingly we shall be obliged to introduce a new postulate, by means of which all the telescoped moods may be dealt with. Thus, the distinction between normal and telescoped moods, though in itself rather trivial and uninteresting, is important because it enables us—or forces us—to give an absolutely complete systematization of our subject. For purposes of strict accuracy and for purposes of ideal completeness, then, we must turn to this somewhat trifling matter of telescoped arguments.

53. Normal versus Telescoped Arguments. By a *telescoped* form of eduction we shall mean one of the form

$$Y_1(s,s) \text{ implies } Y_2(s,s).$$

For example,

$$sEs' \text{ implies } sIs.$$

By a *normal* form of eduction I mean one which is not telescoped. In other words a telescoped form of eduction is one in which the identity of s and p or of s and p' is specified, while a normal form of eduction is one in which the identity of s and p or of s and p' is not specified.

Similarly, a telescoped form of syllogism is one of the form
$$Y_1(s,m) \text{ and } Y_2(s,m) \text{ implies } Y_3(s,s)$$
or of the form
$$Y_1(s,s) \text{ and } Y_2(s,m) \text{ implies } Y_3(s,m) ;$$
and a normal form of syllogism is one which is not telescoped.

Similarly with the sorites.

General definitions of telescoped and normal forms of *argument* are not easy to give, but the following will perhaps serve. A telescoped form of argument (eduction, syllogism, or sorites) is one in which the identity of certain terms is specified, additional to the identities specified in the definitions of eduction, syllogism, or sorites. A normal form of argument is one which does not specify the identity of any terms other than those the identity of which is specified in the definitions of eduction, syllogism, or sorites.

Now, as the reader may easily see from the proved summaries in the foregoing chapters, the validity or invalidity of every *normal* form of eduction, syllogism, or sorites follows from the postulates.

The question naturally arises : is every telescoped form of argument deducibly valid or invalid from the postulates? It is clear of course that some telescoped forms of argument are determined by the postulates. For example, that sEs' implies sIs and that sEs' does not imply sIs' can easily be shown to follow from the postulates. But what of the argument sIs' *implies* sEs', for example? The postulates fail to determine this form of argument. Many other examples could be given of telescoped arguments which do not follow from the postulates and whose invalidity also does not follow from the postulates. Our postulates, therefore, as they stand, are not complete. At least one further postulate is required in order that the theory of telescoped arguments may be completed. In the next section we shall search for the postulate or postulates which will complete our systematization of Aristotelian logic.

54. The Search for a New Postulate. If we consider all the possible moods of telescoped eduction and set ourselves the problem of determining which are to be considered valid and which invalid we shall find that the complete solution of this problem depends upon the answer which we give to the following question : is sEs' true for all values of s?

The same is true of the syllogism and the sorites. As can be shown, if the question just mentioned is answered, a complete account of the telescoped moods of syllogism and sorites is determined.

We need accordingly but one new postulate, and the problem boils down to this : shall the affirmative or the negative answer to the above question be adopted as the new postulate? In other words, which of the two following possible postulates (which we may call 1.51 and 1.52 respectively) shall be added to our system?

 1.51 sEs'

 1.52 There exists an element s such that sEs' *is false.*

Unfortunately there is no certain way of answering. For, in the first place, as we have already implied, neither 1.51 nor 1.52 is deducible from the postulates of Chapter I ; that is to say, considerations of consistency do not require that one of the two principles rather than the other be adopted. In the second place, although a simple and reasonable interpretation of our abstract system can be given such that 1.51 together with all the postulates of Chapter I is satisfied, it is equally the case that another simple and reasonable interpretation will satisfy 1.52 and the postulates of Chapter I. In the third place, the tradition itself—the doctrine of the textbooks—is silent on this matter and leaves us free to choose as we will between 1.51 and 1.52.

This last statement might be disputed. 1.51 is equivalent to sAs ; sAs may be read *All s is s ;* and *All s is s* might be thought to be the traditional " law of identity " : hence one might argue that we are compelled by the tradition to adopt 1.51 rather than 1.52. I maintain, however, that *All s is s* is not the law of identity. The law of identity is rather the principle that *s is s*, which is something quite different. The critic will counter that when one asserts as a principle of logic that *s is s* one means of course to assert it for all values of *s*. And we reply that if we assert as a principle of logic that *All s is s* we also mean to assert *that* for all values of *s* ; *s is s for all values of s* is not the same as *All s is s for all values of s* : in other words, the quantifier *All* in the form *All s is p* has a special technical meaning in traditional logic which is not the same as the " all " by means of which a propositional function may be changed into a general proposition. Furthermore, when the textbooks give an illustration of the law of identity, it is usually " Socrates is Socrates," or something of the sort. In other words, the *s* in the textbooks' law of identity stands for a singular term, whereas the terms of *All s is p* are supposedly general. As a matter of fact, the law of identity in the textbooks is an extremely vague pronouncement; and I therefore feel no obligation to pay any further attention to it in this work.

Neither considerations of consistency, nor of interpretation, nor of tradition, compel us or aid us in endeavouring to choose between 1.51 and 1.52. No other solid criteria remain. Accordingly, if one must choose, the choice will be based merely on personal predilection. Some readers will perhaps prefer 1.51, others 1.52, and others will be quite indifferent.

We shall therefore end this discussion by stating that there are two equally tenable systems of Aristotelian logic. These two systems agree in all respects except in their answers to the rather trivial question whether *sEs'* holds for all values of *s* and in the consequences of their divergent answers to that question.

We have then two alternative sets of postulates, which, for purposes of reference, are stated in the next two sections.

55. Postulate Set A. This set consists of the postulates of Chapter I together with principle 1.52.

1.1 If *s* is an element, *s'* is an element
1.2 *sEp* is equivalent to *sEp''*
1.3 *sEp* implies *s'Ep is false*
1.4 *sEm'* and *pEm* implies *mEp*
1.5 *sEp* implies *pEp'*
1.52 There exists an element *s* such that *sEs' is false*
1.6 There exist elements *s*, *m*, and *p* such that *sEm* and *mEp* and *sEp*

56. Postulate Set B. This set would consist of the postulates of Chapter I together with 1.51, except that 1.53, given below, happens to be more convenient than 1.51. From 1.53 we may deduce 1.51. Also, since 1.5 may be deduced, it is dropped.

1.1   If s is an element, s' is an element
1.2 sEp is equivalent to sEp''
1.3 sEp implies *$s'Ep$ is false*
1.4 sEm' and pEm implies sEp
1.53 *sEp is false* implies pEp'
1.6   There exist elements s, m, and p such that sEm and mEp and sEp

CHAPTER V

DISTRIBUTION, QUALITY, AND QUANTITY[1]

57. Introduction. We turn now to the problem of the rules. The most famous of the rules of traditional logic are those for the syllogism. But rules for conversion, as well as special rules for the sorites, are also included in the tradition. We are enabled by these sets of rules to test given arguments for validity, to infer conclusions from a given premise or given premises, and to supply a premise or set of premises from which a given conclusion may be inferred. These sets of rules constitute a sort of *superstructure* based upon the exposition of forms which we have studied in Chapters I–IV.

The rules are framed in terms of the following concepts: the distribution of terms, the quality of propositions, and the quantity of propositions. In the present chapter we shall analyse these ideas.

We begin with the notion of distribution, which is particularly in need of analysis.

58. The Doctrine of Distribution. The doctrine of distribution, as ordinarily set forth, consists of three points.

First, we have the concept of distribution, which is expressed in a definition. The definition, as ordinarily given, is so vague as to be almost useless. We shall be obliged to supply a more precise definition.

Second, we have the table of distribution, which is supposedly deduced from the definition. According to the table, the following terms, and none others, are distributed by the *A*, *E*, *I*, and *O* forms. The *A* form distributes its subject; the *E* form distributes its subject and predicate; the *O* form distributes its predicate.

[1] The views expressed in this chapter were first published in my article, "Negative Terms in Traditional Logic," *Monist*, Vol. XLII (1932), pp. 96–111.

Third, there is the principle of distribution, which asserts as a general rule of inference that when an argument is valid the terms which are distributed by the conclusion are also distributed by the premises.

59. The Contradiction. Now the doctrine of distribution is flatly inconsistent with other principles of traditional logic. This may be shown as follows.

Take the following form of argument : *sAp implies s'Op*. By the table of distribution, *p* is distributed in the conclusion but is not distributed in the premise. Hence, by the principle of distribution, the argument is invalid. But, as a matter of fact, the argument is valid in traditional logic, as we have seen (Sec. 32). The validity of the argument may be seen alternatively as follows : if one starts with *sAp* and then obverts, simply converts, obverts, converts by limitation, and obverts, one arrives legitimately at the conclusion *s'Op*, which is called the *partial inverse* of *sAp*. Certain logicians, I believe, have felt that the onus of this contradiction should be placed upon inversion, and that that process ought perhaps to be banned from traditional logic. However, one cannot reject inversion without at the same time repudiating either simple conversion, conversion by limitation, or obversion ; for inversion is a mere compound of these three.

Moreover, the contradiction may be exhibited without any mention of inversion. Consider contraposition of the *A* proposition : *sAp implies p'As'*. (That this is valid follows from obversion, simple conversion, and obversion ; or *cf.* Sec. 32.) But *p'*, which is distributed in the conclusion, is not distributed in the premise, according to the table of distribution.

Again, consider obversion. For example : *sAp implies sEp'*. As before, *p'*, though not distributed by the premise, is distributed by the conclusion.

The contradiction, furthermore, is not confined to eduction. Take the mediate argument : *sAm and mAp implies p'As'*, which is valid by *Barbara* and contraposition. Here, once more, *p'* is distributed by the conclusion but is not distributed by a premise. To reply that this argument is " not a syllogism " is beside the point. Whether it be a syllogism or not, it is at least a valid form of argument (by *Barbara* and contraposition); and the principle of distribution professes to be a *general rule of inference*, not a mere technical convenience which holds in some connections but not in others.

There can be no doubt, then, that the doctrine of distribution is inconsistent with the fundamental structure of traditional logic. Our problem is accordingly the following: how can the contradiction be resolved?

60. The Source of the Contradiction. The source of the contradiction is not difficult to find. The contradiction is due to the presence of negative terms in the system (in other words, to obversion, contraposition, and inversion, which make negative terms operative). Before negative terms had been admitted, when simple conversion and conversion by limitation were the only forms of eduction recognized, no such contradiction existed, as can easily be seen.

One might conclude that therefore negative terms have no place in traditional logic. But this inference would be quite indefensible. Negative terms—that is to say, the process of obversion and its compounds—are now firmly incorporated in the tradition. The problem is not how to get rid of them, but how to accommodate them.

The error of the traditional logicians has been to suppose that negative terms may be admitted without any consequent reorganization. We shall see that when negative terms are in the system, certain terms are then distributed by the A, E, I, and O forms which previously were not distributed. The presence of negative terms in the system requires alterations in the table of distribution. When negative terms are in the system a new table of distribution is deducible from the definition of distribution, and by means of this new table we shall be able to eliminate the contradiction.

61. Definition of Distribution. Before we can proceed further, we must clarify and formulate the concept of distribution. The usual definition of distribution is not only unclear but also non-abstract, for it is expressed in terms of a particular interpretation of traditional logic. Now the point of view of the present chapter is entirely abstract; we are endeavouring not to anticipate the results of Chapter VII. Consequently we require a definition which presupposes no interpretation of the A, E, I, and O forms. Accordingly the following definition of distribution, which seeks to render in abstract form the meaning of distribution ordinarily intended, is proposed.

A propositional form f is said to distribute a term a when (and only when) f implies eductively[1] (1) an A form whose subject is a or (2) an E form whose subject is a or (3) an O form whose predicate is a.[2]

This definition might be objected to as follows: it defines distribution in terms of valid eduction; and then in the next chapter we turn around and give rules for eduction in terms of distribution. This procedure is of course circular; but it is not viciously so; and our procedure must and should be circular. For the rules of traditional logic do not pretend to constitute an ultimate *proof* of the validity of certain forms of argument; they are rather *devices* which enable us to test the validity of given arguments and which serve other similar purposes; they constitute a *superstructure*, based upon the structure which we have studied in the preceding chapters.

62. The Old Table of Distribution. Let us now test our definition of distribution by showing that it yields precisely the usual table of distribution. According to our theory, this table is the one which applies when negative terms are not in the system. In deducing this table, we consequently restrict eduction to simple conversion, conversion by limitation, subalternation, and what we may call "repetition."[3]

Now sAp implies eductively the following: sAp, sIp, and pIs. These are the only forms of valid eduction from the A form when negative terms have not been admitted. Consequently, in the system of traditional-logic-without-negative-terms, sAp distributes its subject, but distributes no other term.

[1] A form f is said to "imply eductively" a form g, when "f implies g" is a valid mood of eduction.
[2] A fourth alternative, "an E form whose predicate is a," need not be included, as it is deducible from (2).
[3] "Repetition" is the process of inferring a proposition from itself; *e.g.*, sAp may be inferred from sAp.

Similarly with the other propositional forms: *sEp* implies eductively *sEp, pEs, sOp,* and *pOs,* but no others. Hence *sEp* distributes its subject and its predicate (and these only). *sIp* implies eductively *sIp* and *pIs* alone. Hence *sIp* distributes no term. *sOp* implies eductively only *sOp*. Hence it distributes its predicate but no other term.

Accordingly, when simple conversion, conversion by limitation, subalternation, and repetition are the only forms of eduction recognized, the customary table of distribution follows from our definition.

But, for the system of traditional-logic-*with*-negative-terms, we deduce a different table of distribution. We may call it the new table of distribution. By means of it we shall be able to resolve the contradiction.

63. The New Table of Distribution. When obversion is admitted to traditional logic as a valid form of eduction, the second clause in our definition becomes redundant. We may consequently redefine distribution (for the system of traditional-logic-*with*-negative-terms) as follows: a propositional form *f* is said to distribute a term *a* when (and only when) *f* implies eductively (1) an *A* form whose subject is *a* or (2) an *O* form whose predicate is *a*.

Let us now see what terms are distributed when not only simple conversion, conversion by limitation, subalternation, and repetition, but also obversion and hence contraposition, inversion, etc., are recognized.

sAp implies eductively the following: *sAp, p'As', sEp', p'Es, sIp, sOp', pIs, pOs', s'Ip', s'Op, p'Os,* and *p'Is'*. Hence *sAp* distributes its subject, the contradictory of its subject, its predicate, and the contradictory of its predicate.

sEp implies eductively the following: *sEp, pEs, sAp', pAs', sIp', p'Is, sOp, p'Os', s'Ip, pIs', s'Op', pOs*. Hence *sEp* distributes its subject, the contradictory of its subject, its predicate, and the contradictory of its predicate.

sIp implies eductively the following: *sIp, pIs, sOp',* and *pOs'*. Hence *sIp* distributes the contradictory of its subject and the contradictory of its predicate.

sOp implies eductively the following: *sOp, sIp', p'Is, p'Os'*. Hence *sOp* distributes its predicate, and the contradictory of its subject.

The above results may be summed up as follows:

New Table of Distribution

The following are the terms distributed by the *A, E, I,* and *O* forms:

A : subject, contradictory of subject, predicate, contradictory of predicate ;
E : subject, contradictory of subject, predicate, contradictory of predicate ;
I : contradictory of subject, contradictory of predicate ;
O : contradictory of subject, predicate.

64. Summary and Transition. The contradiction has now been resolved, as the reader may easily verify; and this resolution has been effected without any change in either the concept or the principle of distribution.

However, in view of the large number of terms which are distributed according to the new table, one might suspect that in removing the contradiction we have at the same time destroyed the utility of the notion of distribution.

This suspicion would be correct were it not for the fact that there are *two kinds of distribution*, which we proceed to distinguish.

65. Strong versus Weak Distribution. Since there are two clauses in our definition of distribution, we may distinguish two kinds of distribution. The first may be called *strong distribution* and the second *weak distribution*.

A term *a* is said to be strongly distributed by a propositional form *f* if (and only if) *f* implies eductively an *A* form whose subject is *a*.

A term *a* is said to be weakly distributed by a propositional form *f* if (and only if) *f* implies eductively an *O* form whose predicate is *a*.

To complete our treatment of distribution it remains only to provide tables of strong and of weak distribution.

66. Table of Strong Distribution. The following are the terms which are *strongly distributed* by the A, E, I, and O forms:
A : subject, contradictory of predicate;
E : subject, predicate.
The reader may easily verify this table.

67. Table of Weak Distribution. The terms which are *weakly distributed* by the A, E, I, and O forms are precisely the same as those which are *distributed* by them, as the reader may verify. The table of weak distribution is, in other words, the same as the new table of distribution.

68. Quality and Quality-in-sense. As in the doctrine of distribution, so also in that of quality, the presence of negative terms in the system gives rise to a difficulty.

This may be seen as follows. sAp *implies* sEp' is a valid form of argument. Here the premise, being an A form, is affirmative, and the conclusion, being an E form, is negative. Now, I do not know that an overt contradiction can be imputed to the textbooks on this point. For they perhaps do not intend to assert as a general rule of inference that when the conclusion of an argument is negative at least one premise must be negative. But at least the desirability of effecting certain alterations in this connection is clear.

The old notion of quality may conveniently be retained, but it should be supplemented by a related notion which we may call "quality-in-sense."

In order to define "affirmative-in-sense" and "negative-in-sense" we require the idea of "elements of negativity." By elements of negativity I mean the "No" which heads the E form and the "not" which succeeds the "is" in an O form (in other words the fact that a propositional form is negative is one element of negativity), and each negative term which appears in the proposition (*i.e.* a negative subject is an element of negativity and a negative predicate is an element of negativity).

A propositional form is said to be affirmative-in-sense if it contains an even number of elements of negativity (where zero is regarded as an even number). For example, sAp is affirmative-in-sense, since it contains no element of negativity; $s'Ap'$ and

$s'Ep$ are each affirmative-in-sense, as they contain each two elements of negativity.

A propositional form is said to be negative-in-sense if it contains an odd number of elements of negativity. For example, sEp and sIp', which contain each one element of negativity, are each negative-in-sense; $s'Op'$ is negative-in-sense, for it contains three elements of negativity.

We require also the notions of "together-affirmative-in-sense" and "together-negative-in-sense."

Two or more propositional forms are said to be together-affirmative-in-sense if they contain collectively an even number of elements of negativity (where zero is regarded as even). For example, sEm and mEp are together-affirmative-in-sense.

Two or more propositional forms are said to be together-negative-in-sense if they contain collectively an odd number of elements of negativity. For example, sEm and mAp.

69. Quantity. The notion of quantity is obviously not affected by the presence of negative terms in the system, and requires no further discussion.

CHAPTER VI

THE RULES OF ARISTOTELIAN LOGIC

70. Introduction to Rules for Eduction. The textbooks provide us with a set of so-called " rules for conversion." These rules have a wider significance than their name suggests. They are, as a matter of fact, rules for *eduction* in the system of traditional-logic-*without*-negative-terms. That is to say, before negative terms had been introduced into traditional logic, " eduction " meant an argument of the form:
$$X_1(s,p) \text{ implies } X_2(s,p).[1]$$
Using the old table of distribution, one finds that these rules constitute a set of necessary and sufficient conditions for the validity of eduction so defined.

But when negative terms are admitted the meaning of eduction is extended. We now mean by eduction an argument of the form
$$Y_1(s,p) \text{ implies } Y_2(s,p).$$
Now the old rules do not constitute an adequate test of all arguments of that form. Hence a new set of rules ought to be given : a set of rules for eduction in the system-of-traditional-logic-*with*-negative-terms.

Such a set of rules is not only desirable for the sake of completeness ; it is necessary for the sake of consistency. For, when negative terms are in the system, the table of distribution must be extended, as we have seen, and, if one uses the new table of distribution—as one must when negative terms are in the system—the old rules no longer constitute an adequate test of conversion. Thus, if the new table of distribution be used, the invalid argument *sAp implies pAs* satisfies all of the old rules.

Accordingly, our next task will be to construct a set of rules for eduction in the system of traditional-logic-*with*-negative-terms, that is to say, the system of traditional logic as it now exists.

[1] For the explanation of these symbols see Sec. 21.

Thanks to our discussion in the preceding chapter, such a set—a set which tests all eductions whether or not they contain negative terms—may be given immediately. It is framed in terms of quality-in-sense and distribution. (The new table of distribution, of course, is to be used.)

71. Rules for Eduction.[1] A form of eduction is valid if and only if it satisfies all of the following conditions :

1. If the conclusion is affirmative-in-sense, the premise is affimative-in-sense.

2. If the conclusion is negative-in-sense, the premise is negative-in-sense.

3. If the conclusion is universal, the terms which are strongly distributed by the conclusion are strongly distributed by the premise.

4. If the conclusion is particular, the terms which are distributed by the conclusion are distributed by the premise.

For the proof that these rules are necessary and sufficient see Sec. 74.

The independence of these four rules may be shown as follows. The invalid argument sEp implies sIp (2.51) violates rule 1, but none of the other rules. The invalid argument sEp' implies sIp' (2.51, p'/p) violates rule 2, but none of the others. The invalid argument sEp implies $s'Ep'$ (2.53) violates rule 3, but none of the others. The invalid argument sIp implies $s'Ip'$ (2.54) violates rule 4, but none of the others.

Though these rules are independent, they do not attain the maximum of logical economy : they employ an unnecessarily large equipment of concepts. Accordingly the following alternative set of rules, which is logically simpler, is proposed. It dispenses with the somewhat barbarous notion of quality-in-sense and is framed entirely in terms of distribution.

---

[1] The rules given in Secs. 71, 72, and 73 are rules for *normal* eduction (Sec. 53). The rules of the present section were first published in my article, " Negative Terms in Traditional Logic," *Monist*, Vol. XLII (1932), pp. 96–111.

72. Second Set of Rules for Eduction.[1] A form of eduction is valid if (and only if) the dyad, consisting of the premise of the eduction and the contradictory of the conclusion of the eduction, satisfies the following conditions:

1. Of the two propositional forms which constitute the dyad, both are universal, or one is particular and one universal.

2. If both are universal, one and only one of the terms which is strongly distributed by one of the two propositional forms is strongly distributed by the other.

3. If one is particular and one universal, neither of the terms which are distributed by the particular is strongly distributed by the universal.

For the proof that these rules are necessary and sufficient see Sec. 74.

I now wish to give another alternative set of rules for eduction. This next set will dispense with both the notions of quality-in-sense and distribution, and will be expressed by means of the notion of quantity and the " agreement " and " disagreement " of terms.

73. Third Set of Rules for Eduction. A form of eduction is valid if (and only if) the dyad, consisting of an E or I form which is eductively equivalent[2] to the premise and an E or I form which is eductively equivalent to the contradictory of the conclusion, satisfies the following conditions:

1. Of the two propositional forms which constitute the dyad, both are universal, or one is particular and one is universal.

2. If both are universal, a term of the one agrees with a term of the other, and a term of the one disagrees with a term of the other.[3]

3. If one is particular and one universal, both the terms of the one agree with the terms of the other.

For the proof that these rules are necessary and sufficient see Sec. 74.

---

[1] The form in which this set of rules is expressed is of course influenced by Mrs. Ladd-Franklin's " antilogism." Similarly with the rules given in Secs. 73, 78, 79, 83, and 84.
[2] Cf. Sec. 24.
[3] For the meaning of the " agreement " and " disagreement " of terms, see Sec. 47 (5).

74. Proof of the Rules for Eduction. Let us begin with the third set of rules. Their necessity and sufficiency may be shown as follows. The first step in the proof consists of pointing out that each one of the valid moods 2.41, 2.42, and 2.44 satisfies all of the rules and that each one of the moods declared invalid by 2.51–2.59 violates one of the three rules, as the reader may easily verify. Now, as we have seen (Sec. 33), every valid eduction whose premise is either an E or an I form and whose conclusion is either an E or an I form is derivable from some one of the three moods 2.41, 2.42, and 2.44 by term substitution, or by simple conversion of premise or conclusion. But, obviously, neither term substitution nor simple conversion affects the number of pairs of terms which agree nor the number which disagree, nor the quantity of the propositional forms. Hence every valid eduction whose premise is either E or I and whose conclusion is either E or I satisfies the rules. Similarly every invalid eduction whose premise is either E or I and whose conclusion is either E or I violates at least one rule. Finally, as we have seen, every eduction is equivalent to one whose premise is E or I and whose conclusion is E or I; and the rules provide that an eduction whose premise is A or O, or whose conclusion is A or O, stands or falls with an equivalent eduction whose premise is E or I and whose conclusion is E or I. Hence every valid mood of eduction satisfies the rules; and every invalid mood violates at least one rule; and the rules accordingly are necessary and sufficient.

The second set of rules is obviously equivalent to the third set, by the new table of distribution. Hence the necessity and sufficiency of the second set.

Finally, the first set is a sufficient set of necessary rules; for the first set is equivalent to the second, as can be shown.

75. Concerning Rules for Telescoped Eduction. The foregoing sets of rules apply only to *normal*[1] forms of eduction. Rules for telescoped forms of eduction may be formulated easily. As they have but slight interest they are omitted. Of course, rules for telescoped eduction based upon Postulate Set A will not be equivalent to rules based upon Postulate Set B.[2]

[1] For the distinction between "normal" and "telescoped" forms see Sec. 52.
[2] For Sets A and B see Secs. 55–6.

76. Introduction to Rules for the Syllogism. The standard treatment of the syllogism was worked out before negative terms had been admitted into the system. Consequently " syllogism " meant an argument of the form

$$X_1(s,m) \text{ and } X_2(m,p) \text{ implies } X_3(s,p).[1]$$

The standard or old rules for the syllogism are based upon the old table of distribution and are necessary and sufficient conditions for the validity of syllogism so defined.

But when negative terms have been admitted the meaning of syllogism should be extended and it should be defined as argument of the form

$$Y_1(s,m) \text{ and } Y_2(m,p) \text{ implies } Y_3(s,p).$$

But the old rules fail to provide an adequate test for syllogism thus defined, even when the new table is employed. Hence a new set of rules is required.

We shall give three alternative sets of rules for the syllogism, which correspond to our three sets of rules for eduction.

77. Rules for the Syllogism.[2] A syllogistic form is valid if (and only if) it satisfies all of the following conditions :

1. If the conclusion is affirmative-in-sense, the premises are together-affirmative-in-sense.

2. If the conclusion is negative-in-sense, the premises are together-negative-in-sense.

3. If the conclusion is universal, the terms which it strongly distributes are strongly distributed by the premises.

4. If the conclusion is particular :

(*a*) the terms which are distributed by the conclusion are distributed by the premises ;

(*b*) at least one of the terms distributed by the conclusion is strongly distributed by the premises.

The independence of these rules may be shown by the following examples. The syllogistic forms declared invalid by theorems 3.34, 3.35, 3.422, 3.36, and 3.31 violate respectively rules 1, 2, 3, 4a, and 4b only.

---

[1] For the explanation of these symbols see Sec. 21.
[2] The rules given in Secs. 77, 78, and 79 are rules for *normal* forms of syllogism (Sec. 53). The rules of the present section were first published in my article, " Negative Terms in Traditional Logic," *Monist*, Vol. XLII, pp. 96–111.

It is interesting to note that in this set of rules no middle term rule is required.

78. Second Set of Rules for the Syllogism. A syllogistic form is valid if (and only if) the triad, consisting of its premises and the contradictory of its conclusion, satisfies the following conditions :

1. Of the three propositional forms which constitute the triad, all three are universal, or two are universal and one is particular.

2. If all three are universal, one and only one term is strongly distributed twice.

3. If two are universal and one is particular, neither of the terms which is distributed by the particular is strongly distributed by the universals, and no term (of the universals) is strongly distributed twice.

79. Third Set of Rules for the Syllogism. A syllogistic form is valid if (and only if) the triad, consisting of E or I forms which are eductively equivalent to the premises and an E or I form which is eductively equivalent to the contradictory of the conclusion, satisfies the following conditions :

1. Of the three propositional forms which constitute the triad, all three are universal, or two are universal and one is particular.

2. If all three are universal, one and only one pair of terms agrees.[1]

3. If two are universal and one is particular, both terms of the particular agree with terms of the universals and a term of one universal disagrees with a term of the other universal.[1]

80. Proof of the Rules for Syllogism. The proof that our rules for the syllogism are necessary and sufficient is strictly analogous to our proof of the rules of eduction and may be omitted.

81. Introduction to Rules for the Sorites. The same reasons which require new rules for eduction and syllogism require new

---

[1] For the meaning of the " agreement " and " disagreement " of terms see Sec. 47 (4 and 5).

rules for the sorites which will be applicable whether or not the sorites contains negative terms.

82. Rules for the Sorites. A set of rules corresponding to the first set for eduction and syllogism (*i.e.* expressed in terms of distribution and quality-in-sense) can be given. But it is extremely cumbrous and is therefore omitted. We pass on immediately to sets of rules corresponding to the second and third sets for eduction and syllogism.

83. Second Set of Rules for Sorites.[1] A sorites is valid if (and only if) the polyad, consisting of its premises and the contradictory of its conclusion, satisfies the following conditions :

1. Of the propositional forms which constitute the polyad, all are universal, or one is particular and all but one are universal.

2. If all are universal, one and only one term is strongly distributed twice.

3. If one and only one is particular, neither of the terms which is distributed by the particular is strongly distributed by the universals, and no term is strongly distributed twice.

84. Third Set of Rules for Sorites. A sorites is valid if (and only if) the polyad, consisting of E or I forms which are eductively equivalent to the premises and an E or I form which is eductively equivalent to the contradictory of the conclusion, satisfies the following conditions :

1. Of the propositional forms which constitute the polyad, all are universal, or one and only one is particular.

2. If all are universal, one and only one pair of terms agrees.[2]

3. If one and only one is particular, both terms of the particular agree with terms of two of the universals and a term in each universal disagrees with a term in another universal.[2]

85. Proof of the Rules for the Sorites. The rules are equivalent to the summary of the sorites (Secs. 48 and 50), as can be shown. Hence the rules are necessary and sufficient.

---

[1] These rules as well as those in the next section are for *normal* forms of sorites. For the meaning of " normal " see Sec. 53.
[2] For the meaning of the " agreement " and " disagreement " of terms see Sec. 47 (4 and 5).

86. General Rules of Inference. The rules for the sorites can easily be reworded in such a way that they constitute a set of necessary and sufficient conditions for the validity not only of sorites and syllogism but of eduction as well.

87. Telescoped Syllogism and Telescoped Sorites. Rules for telescoped[1] syllogism and for telescoped sorites can be given, but, as they have little interest, they are omitted.

---

[1] For the meaning of "telescoped" see Sec. 52.

CHAPTER VII

INTERPRETATIONS OF ARISTOTELIAN LOGIC

88. Introduction. In the preceding chapters our point of view was entirely abstract. We were concerned with the bare symbols s, m, p, s', m', p', sAp, sEp, sIp, and sOp. It is true that we allowed ourselves the liberty of unofficially " reading " these symbols in a special way. Thus s, m, p, etc. were called the " terms " of categorical propositions. s' was read *non-s ;* and sAp, sEp, sIp, and sOp were read *All s is p*, *No s is p*, etc. But, as we indicated, the meaning of these readings was left indeterminate, so that even when we used them our point of view was still really abstract.

The problem of the present chapter is to give an accurate and explicit meaning to our symbols—or to our " readings."

There are two ways in which we might look for an interpretation of our abstract system. On the one hand we might begin by trying to find the " real " or " correct " meaning of our fundamental undefined idea *No s is p*. On the other hand we might proceed on the assumption that it is largely a matter of convention what meaning we choose for *No s is p;* consequently we should adopt a trial and error method, assigning sets of meanings experimentally to our assumed ideas until we should find one which would make our postulates true.

Now I maintain that the search for a uniquely " correct " meaning for *No s is p* is hopeless. Who has the temerity to claim an insight so penetrating and so exhaustive that it reveals one and only one meaning for the universal negative enthroned in the Platonic heaven? The only possible way of substantiating the doctrine that the expression *No s is p* has a single " real " meaning would be to appeal to the usage of ordinary discourse. But speech forms are fluid. Their meanings vary from context to context. And even if language were dryly unambiguous, the logician could still claim the right to redefine for scientific purposes.

Accordingly, our problem in this chapter is not that of questing for any absolute. It is rather the modest task of finding an interpretation *which will fit* our abstract system, and which at the same time will have *some* foundation in ordinary speech.

89. The Search for an Interpretation. We shall begin our search for an interpretation of traditional logic by noting the most general sense in which the word " class " might be understood —for we shall find it convenient to treat the elements of the system as classes—and the most general meaning which might be attached to the expression *No s is p*. If these most general meanings fail to work in traditional logic, we may continue our search by gradually specializing either or both of these two meanings.

The most general significance of which the word " class " is susceptible is one in accordance with which we may speak consistently of *a class which has no members and of a class the membership of which coincides with the entire universe of discourse*. For example, " mathematicians who have squared the circle," though of course there *are* none, will constitute a class, on this view. Similarly, " beings who are *not* mathematicians-who-have-squared-the-circle " will constitute a class, even though this class exhausts the universe. A class with no members is called a *null class*. A class the membership of which coincides with the universe of discourse may be called a *universe class*.

The rigorous defining of this conception of class is a complicated matter. We may give, however, the following rough definition. By a " class " we mean those entities which satisfy a propositional function, whether or not there are any, and whether or not there are any which do not satisfy it. By a " propositional function " is meant an expression which contains one or more variables and which becomes a proposition when the variables are replaced by values. For example, " x is human " is a propositional function ; when " x " is replaced by the value " John " we have a true proposition ; when " x " is replaced by the value " Fido " we have a false proposition. By the entities which *satisfy* a propositional function we mean those values which, when they replace the variable, give rise to true propositions. Thus the class of men is precisely those entities which satisfy the propositional function " x is human."

The most general meaning which can reasonably be assigned to *No s is p* is the following : " the logical product of *s* and *p* is null " (*i.e.* the class consisting of the objects which are members of *both s* and *p* is null); this may be expressed, alternatively, " *s* is included in *non-p*." If this is the meaning of *No s is p*, the other classical forms will have the following meanings. *All s is p* will mean " the logical product of *s* and *non-p* is null " (alternatively, " *s* is included in *p* "). *Some s is p* will mean " the logical product of *s* and *p* is not null " (alternatively, " *s* is not included in *non-p* "). *Some s is not p* will mean " the logical product of *s* and *non-p* is not null " (alternatively, " *s* is not included in *p* ").

Now these meanings of " class " and of *No s is p* and the other forms are of course the ones employed in the *modern* logic of classes. And, as is well known, if all these meanings be assigned, traditional logic will not hold. Why these most general meanings will not fit traditional logic is easy to see. Among the forms of argument recognized as valid by traditional logic are forms in which the premises are all universal and the conclusion particular. Thus, in traditional logic, *sEp* implies *sOp*. But, on our most general meanings, *sEp* may be true simply because *s* is a null class. In that case, though *sEp* is true, *sOp* would be false and hence *sEp* would not imply *sOp*. In short, if *s*, *m*, *p*, etc., be interpreted as meaning " classes " in the modern sense, and if *sEp* and the other propositional forms be given the most general meanings just explained, then none of the traditionally valid forms of argument which involve the passage from universal premises to a particular conclusion, will hold.

Accordingly to find an interpretation which will fit traditional logic, we must narrow either the meaning of " class," or the meaning of *sEp* and the other propositional forms. Previous searches for an interpretation of traditional logic have all, so far as I am aware, retained the most general meaning of class, while restricting the meaning of one or more of the propositional forms. This of course is one good way of proceeding. In fact in this way we can arrive at an interpretation which will satisfy all the postulates of Set A. In looking for an interpretation of

Set A in this manner we must, however, avoid the mistakes committed by many previous investigators, who have made either or both of the following blunders. First, while complicating the meaning of *sEp* and *sAp*, they have retained the simple modern meaning of *sIp* and *sOp*; as a result the oppositional principles of contradiction are not satisfied. Second, they have complicated the meanings of *sEp* and *sAp* incorrectly; consequently, while they have succeeded in validating certain forms of traditional argument, they have failed to validate all of them. As a result of these mistakes, no previously proposed interpretation, so far as I know, has satisfied all of the postulates of set A. We may easily avoid these errors as follows. Since *sAp*, *sIp*, and *sOp* do not appear in the postulates, let us try out various possible meanings of *sEp* until we find one which satisfies all of the postulates. The meanings of *sAp*, *sIp*, and *sOp* will thereby be determined, since they are defined (1.91–1.93) in terms of *sEp*. Proceeding in this manner we arrive at the interpretation given in the next section.

90. Interpretation A. If the following meanings be assigned to our assumed ideas, all of the postulates of Set A will be satisfied.

1. By the elements of the system, symbolized by small letters of the alphabet, we shall mean " classes " (in the modern sense).

2. By *s'* we shall mean the class *non-s*.

3. By *sEp* we shall mean *s is included in non-p, and s is not null, and p is not null*.

From (3) and definitions 1.91–1.93, it follows that the meanings of *sAp*, *sIp*, and *sOp* are:

sAp will mean *s is included in p, and s is not null, and non-p is not null*.

sIp will mean *s is not included in non-p, or s is null, or p is null*.

sOp will mean *s is not included in p, or s is null, or non-p is null*.

I now wish to show that the above interpretation satisfies all the postulates of Set A and also that it is the *only* non-redundant interpretation which can be arrived at " in the usual way " which does satisfy them all. By " the usual way " I mean adopting the meanings (1) and (2) above and letting *sEp* mean a conjunction of propositions one of which is "*s* is included in *non-p*" and the other or others of which is one or more of the propositions "*s* is not null," "*non-s* is not null," "*p* is not null," and "*non-p* is not null."

This can best be shown by means of the following table. The symbols in the left-hand column will represent various proposed meanings of *sEp* arrived at "in the usual way." To save space these proposed meanings are written in abbreviated form: thus "s" will stand for the interpretation "*s* is included in *non-p* and *s* is not null"; in other words, it is understood in each case that the interpretation in question is arrived at "in the usual way," and the letter or letters written down will indicate which terms are declared to be not null by the interpretation in question. The other columns will stand for the various postulates of set A; "+" will mean that the interpretation in question satisfies the postulate in whose column "+" is written, and "−" will mean that it fails to satisfy that postulate.

	Interpretation	1.1	1.2	1.3	1.4	1.5	1.52	1.6
(1)	s	+	+	−	+	−	+	+
(2)	s'	+	+	−	+	−	+	+
(3)	p	+	+	+	−	−	+	+
(4)	p'	+	+	−	+	−	+	+
(5)	s s'	+	+	−	+	−	+	+
(6)	s p	+	+	+	+	+	+	+
(7)	s p'	+	+	−	+	−	+	+
(8)	s' p	+	+	+	−	−	+	+
(9)	s' p'	+	+	−	+	−	+	+
(10)	p p'	+	+	+	−	+	+	+
(11)	s s' p	+	+	+	+	+	+	+
(12)	s s' p'	+	+	−	+	−	+	+
(13)	s p p'	+	+	+	+	+	+	+
(14)	s' p p'	+	+	+	−	+	+	+
(15)	s s' p p'	+	+	+	+	+	+	+

From the above table it can be seen that interpretations 6, 11, 13, and 15 are the only ones (arrived at "in the usual way") which satisfy the postulates. But 11, 13, and 15 are simply redundant equivalents of 6. Hence 6 is the only satisfactory non-redundant interpretation. It follows also that meanings assigned to sAp, sIp, and sOp in accordance with 6 are the only satisfactory non-redundant renderings of them.

91. Interpretation B. Of the fifteen possible meanings of sEp arrived at " in the usual way," none will satisfy all the postulates of Set B, as can easily be seen. Accordingly, to find an interpretation of our assumed ideas which will satisfy Set B we must proceed in some way other than the " usual " one.

We have seen that there are two obvious ways of looking for an interpretation of our assumed ideas. One is that of limiting the most general meaning of sEp, the other is that of limiting the most general meaning of " class." Proceeding in the first manner we have found an interpretation of Set A. Proceeding in the second manner we arrive easily at the following interpretation, which satisfies all the postulates of Set B.

1. By the elements of the system we shall mean " classes " in the following *narrower* sense. A class is those entities which satisfy a propositional function, provided that there is at least one entity which does satisfy the function and at least one entity which does not satisfy the function. (According to this narrower conception of " class," we cannot speak consistently of a " null class " or a " universe class.")

2. By s' we shall mean the class (in the narrower sense) *non-s*.

3. By sEp we shall mean *s is included in non-p*.

From (3) and the definitions, it follows that the meanings of sAp, sIp, and sOp are:

sAp : *s is included in p*
sIp : *s is not included in non-p*
sOp : *s is not included in p*

On this interpretation, sEp, sAp, sIp, sOp retain the meaning which they have in modern logic : it is the conception of class which is restricted.

That all of the postulates of Set B are satisfied by this interpretation can easily be verified by the reader. This interpretation of course does not satisfy Set A.

It might be objected that in this interpretation we are making an improper use of "class." But the modern conception of "class" is no more sacred than the modern conception of *No s is p*. The meaning we are to give to the word "class" is just as much a matter of convention as the meaning we are to give to the words *No s is p*. For the purposes of modern logic it is convenient to give the word "class" a wide meaning; for our present purposes it is convenient to give it a narrow meaning.

92. Other Proposed Interpretations. Other interpretations of traditional logic have been proposed by various writers. Bu all that I have ever seen fail at crucial points except one inter pretation which was discovered by Professor Smith.[1] This very important interpretation, which may be found on page 47 of his *System of Formal Logic* and on page 61 of his *Symbolic Logic*, possesses one advantage over the two interpretations proposed in the present work: namely, the modern logic of classes is derivable from traditional logic as interpreted by Professor Smith. On the other hand our interpretations are recommended by their greater simplicity.

93. Extension and Intension. In one important respect our interpretations fall short of complete explicitness. I wish now to remedy that defect.

We have failed to state whether they are to be understood *extensionally* or *intensionally*. We may make them entirely explicit by indicating an extensional version and an intensional version of each interpretation.

The distinction between extension and intension may be introduced into our interpretations in more than one way. The following is perhaps the simplest.

We can make both the first and the second interpretation explicitly extensional by stating simply that when we say "classes" we mean "classes in extension" (*i.e.* classes of *actual* entities). Similarly we can make both explicitly intensional by stating that when we say "classes" we mean "classes in intension" (*i.e.* classes of *possible* entities). No further revision need be made.

---

[1] This interpretation satisfies our Postulate Set B.

The extensional and intensional versions correspond precisely with each other. Where traditional logic taken in extension requires that certain classes have actual members in order that the weakened forms of argument may hold, taken in intension it requires that the same classes have possible members in order that the weakened forms of argument may hold.

CONCLUSION

94. Introduction. We have now solved the three problems which we proposed at the beginning. We have presented traditional logic in the form of a deductive system. We have freed the rules of traditional logic from inconsistency, and have made them adequate to all the forms of traditional argument. We have given an interpretation—indeed more than one interpretation—for our primitive ideas such that all of our postulates hold.

The solution of these problems enables us to answer certain general questions concerning traditional logic.

95. Negative Terms in Aristotelian Logic. Since we have devoted a great deal of attention to " negative terms " throughout this book, let us raise the general question " what is the status of negative terms in traditional logic ? "

Negative terms, and the processes of inference which make them operative, were not admitted to traditional logic, that is to say, were not recognized by the generality of traditional logicians, until rather recently, namely, in the nineteenth century. That they could be admitted without any consequent reorganization of the system was wrongly supposed by logicians. Their presence in the system requires various developments for the sake of completeness and consistency. We have carried out those developments in this book. From one point of view our work may be regarded as an experiment the purpose of which has been to find out whether negative terms can be treated completely and consistently in traditional logic, or whether they are refractory elements which cannot be absorbed and hence must be rejected. The result of the experiment has been to show by actually absorbing negative terms that they can be absorbed.

Though negative terms are thus capable of fitting harmoniously into the system, one might argue that they are not worth all the trouble which they cause, and that it would be better to return to the earlier tradition and repudiate the decision of the nineteenth and twentieth-century logicians who have made negative terms part of the tradition. This would be, it seems to me, an unwarranted and undesirable reaction. For negative terms are of great advantage to traditional logic. On the one hand they increase the power and scope of the system. On the other hand they result in a genuine simplification of the system. Superficially, indeed, negative terms, since their presence requires that all sorts of new distinctions be made, appear to complicate rather than simplify. Yet traditional logic with negative terms is logically simpler than traditional logic without them. When negative terms are admitted, we require only seven postulates, as we have seen, to formulate the whole system. For traditional logic without negative terms, we require about twice as many. Again, when negative terms are in the system, the number of *types* of argument is reduced greatly. For example, in traditional logic with negative terms the various forms of valid eduction are of three fundamental types, and of invalid eduction nine. But in the system without negative terms, there are six types of valid eduction, and fifteen types of invalid eduction. Thus, though the number of moods is increased by the presence of negative terms, the number of types of moods is decreased; so we have at once a gain in comprehensiveness and in logical simplicity. Moreover, the rules of traditional logic with negative terms are at once more powerful and simpler than the old rules: more powerful since they test a wider range of forms of argument, and simpler since they require a smaller apparatus of concepts.

Finally, though the simplest interpretation of traditional-logic-with-negative-terms (our Interpretation B, given in Sec. 91) is no simpler than the simplest interpretation of traditional-logic-without-negative-terms, it involves no loss in simplicity. As a matter of fact, the simplest interpretation of traditional logic with negative terms is identical with the simplest interpretation of traditional logic without negative terms. In the matter of interpretation, then, negative terms entail no loss of simplicity, and in the matter of the rules and the postulates they result in noteworthy gains in simplicity.

96. The Correctness of Aristotelian Logic. Another general question, which we may now answer, is this: " Is traditional logic a *correct* system of logic ? " Perhaps we should *dispose* of the question rather than *answer* it, for it is a rather silly question. We should not need to raise it at all, were it not for the fact that the impression seems to prevail in certain quarters that traditional logic is somehow *wrong*, that the doctrines of traditional logic are not merely restricted principles which fall short of complete generality, but are actually *erroneous*.

What could it mean to say that traditional logic is " wrong " ? It would have to mean that traditional logic is self-contradictory, or that it is a merely abstract system for which no logical interpretation is possible, or that it is a chaotic set of doctrines essentially incapable of systematic formulation. But that traditional logic is none of these things we have shown. We have shown by systematizing it that it can be systematized. We have shown by interpreting it that it can be interpreted. And finally that it is a consistent system follows from the fact that it can be given a true interpretation, for no self-contradictory system can be truly interpreted. The only possible remaining charge of inconsistency would have to do with the rules, the so-called superstructure. But, as we have shown, the errors which traditional logicians have imported into the superstructure are inadvertent ones only, which can be removed without doing violence to the spirit of the subject.

The imputation of incorrectness concerns especially the traditional admission of the " weakened forms " of argument. The critic points to the traditional principle that *All s is p implies Some s is p*, with the comment that of course as a matter of fact *All s is p* does *not* imply *Some s is p*. He forgets to consider that whether or not *All s is p* implies *Some s is p* depends upon the meaning attached to these expressions. If they be given the meanings which we have proposed, then *All s is p* does imply *Some s is p*. The validity or invalidity of the weakened forms is a matter of convention only. The conventions of traditional logic are such that in traditional logic the weakened forms are properly regarded as valid.

97. Aristotelian versus Modern Logic. Finally we may turn to the question : What is the relation of traditional logic to modern logic ?

CONCLUSION

It is sometimes supposed that traditional and modern logic are two rival systems of logic, that if one is " correct " the other must be " incorrect," that if one be " accepted " the other must be " rejected."

I think we can now see that that supposition is quite unjustified. Traditional logic and modern logic are in perfect agreement with each other. The apparent disagreements between them reflect merely a difference of vocabulary. Either " class " or *No s is p*, is given a different meaning in one system from that which it has in the other. But this difference is one of convention only. All the principles of traditional logic can be expressed in the language of modern logic; when so expressed they are principles of modern logic.

Modern logic is of course a much more extensive system than traditional logic. Nothing in traditional logic corresponds to the modern logic of relations, nor to the modern logic of unanalysed propositions. Traditional logic is concerned simply with the logic of classes. But it does not treat even that branch of logic in its full generality. On the one hand it confines itself to a restricted conception of " class " (or of *No s is p*). On the other hand it does not deal with logical sums and products of classes.

Traditional logic thus coincides with part of modern logic—but with part only. It is genuinely a part of Logic—but only a part. It is a special case.

INDEX

References are to sections. Numbers in boldface indicate sections in which terms are defined.

A, 9(a), **19**, Ch. VII
Affirmative, 9(a); *affirmative-in-sense*, **68**
Agreement, of terms, **47**
Aristotle, 1, 5, 10

Categories, 2
Classification, and division, 2
Contradictories, 9(d), 26, 28, **36**
Contraries, 9(d), **36**
Conversion, 9(c); by limitation, 9(c); rules for, 6, 9(f), 70; simple, 9(c)
Correspondents, **36**
Creighton, J. E., 1 n.

Definition, rules of, 2
Dictum de omni et nullo, 10
Disagreement, of terms, **47**
Distribution, 6, 9(e), **61**, **63**, 57–67; strong, **65**, 66; weak, **65**, 67

E, 9(a), Ch. VII.
Eduction, 9(c), **29**, 29–33, 70–75; invalid forms of, 31–33; rules for, 6, 9(f), 70–75; valid forms of, 30, 32, 33; *eductive equivalence*, **24**, 28; *eductive implication*, **61** n.
Enthymeme, 2
Equivalence, **11**, 28; eductive, **24**, 28
Existential import, of propositions, Ch. VII
Extension, 93

Fallacies, 2, 9 (j)

Harrison, C. T., Preface
Henle, Paul, Preface

Hibben, J. G., 1 n.
Huntingdon, E. V., 11

I, 9(a), **19**, Ch. VII
Identity, law of, 54; *identification of terms*, **31**
Implication, 11; eductive, **61** n.
Inference, general rules of, 86; immediate, 9(b), Ch. II; mediate, 9(b), Ch. III
Intension, 93
Interpretation, 7, Ch. VII

Jevons, W. S., 1 n.
Joseph, H. W. B., 1 n.

Ladd-Franklin, C., 72 n.
Langer, S. K., Preface
Leonard, H. S., Preface
Lewis, C. I., Preface, 11
Logic, modern, 1, 8, 97

Negative, propositions, 9(a); terms, 3, 6, 9(c) n., 60, 95; *double negation*, **26**, 28; *elements of negativity*, **68**; *negative-in-sense*, **68**
Normal, forms of argument, **53**

O, 9(a), **19**, Ch. VII
Obversion, 9(c)
Opposition, of propositions, 9(d), **34**, 34–36; of terms, 31

Particular, 9(a)
Postulates, 14–18, 54–56; *postulational method*, 5, 10, 11
Predicables, 2
Predicate, 9(a)

96

THE STRUCTURE OF ARISTOTELIAN LOGIC 97

Premise, 9(b) ; elimination of, 47 ; major, 9(g), 47 ; middle, 47 ; minor, 9(g), 47

Propositions, A, E, I, and *O,* 9(a), 19, Ch. VII ; affirmative, 9(a) ; affirmative-in-sense, 68 ; contradictory, 9(d), 26, 28, 36 ; contrary, 9(d), 36 ; correspondent, 36 ; disjunctive, 2 ; existential import of, Ch. VII ; hypothetical, 2 ; logic of, 1, 11, 97 ; negative, 9(a) ; negative-in-sense, 68 ; opposition of, 9(d), 34, 34-36 ; particular, 9(a) ; subalternate, 9(d), 36 ; subcontrary, 9(d), 36 ; superalternate, 36 ; supplementary, 36 ; universal, 9(a)

Quality, 9(a), 68 ; *quality-in-sense,* 68
Quantity, 9(a), 69

Reduction, of imperfect figures, 10
Relations, logic of, 1, 97
Repetition, 62 n.
Rosinger, K. E., Preface
Rules, 6 ; for conversion, 6, 9(f), 70 ; for eduction, 6, 9(f), 70-75 ; for sorites, 6, 9(k), 81-85, 87 ; for syllogism, 6, 9(j), 76-80, 87
Russell, B., 6

sAp, 9(a), 19, Ch. VII
Sellars, R. W., 1 n.
sEp, 9(a), Ch. VII
Singer, E. A., Jr., Preface, 7, 10 n., 21 n., 30 n., 31, 33 n., 45
sIp, 9(a), 19, Ch. VII
Smith, H. B., Preface, 7, 10 n., 21 n., 45 n., 92
sOp, 9(a), 19, Ch. VII
Sorites, 9(k), 43, 42-51, 81-85, 87 ; invalid forms of, 45, 50 ; rules for, 6, 9(k), 81-85, 87 ; valid forms of, 44, 48

Subalterns, 9(d), 36 ; *subalternation,* 1 15, Ch. VII
Subcontraries, 9(d), 36
Subject, 9(a)
Substitution, 23, 31
Superalternates, 36
Supplementaries, 36
sXp, 21
Syllogism, 9(g), 9(h), 9(i), 9(j), 37, 37-38, 40-41, 76-80, 87 ; figure of, 9(h) ; invalid forms of, 40-41 ; rules for, 6, 9(j), 76-80, 87 ; valid forms of, 9(i), 38, 41
sYp, 21
sZp, 21

Telescoped, forms of argument, 53, Ch. IV, 75, 87
Terms, agreement of, 47 ; disagreement of, 47 ; distribution of, 6, 9(e), 61, 63, 57-67 ; identification of, 31 ; major, 9(g), 47 ; middle, 9(g), 47 ; minor, 9(g), 47 ; negative, 3, 6, 9(c) n., 60, 95 ; opposition of, 31 ; pair of, 47
Type, 33

Universal, 9(a)

Whately, R., 1 n.
Whitehead, A. N., 11
Wolf, A., 1 n.

$X(s, p)$, 21

$Y(s, p)$, 21

$Z(s, p)$, 21